MOTHER ANGELICA
ON PRAYER AND
LIVING FOR THE
KINGDOM

Also by Mother Angelica:

Praying with Mother Angelica
Meditations on the Rosary,
the Way of the Cross,
and Other Prayers

Mother Angelica's
Answers, Not Promises

Mother Angelica on
Christ and Our Lady

Mother Angelica on
Suffering and Burnout

Mother Angelica's Quick
Guide to the Sacraments

MOTHER ANGELICA ON PRAYER AND LIVING FOR THE KINGDOM

EWTN PUBLISHING, INC.
Irondale, Alabama

CONTENTS

The Good Life

MOTHER ANGELICA
ON PRAYER AND
LIVING FOR THE
KINGDOM

EDITOR'S NOTE

This volume brings together for the first time *Living Prayer*, *Journey into Prayer*, *Sharing God Together*, *Rambling Thoughts*, *No Greater Love*, *Jesus My Savior*, *The Gift of Life: He Chose Me to Be*, *Sympathetic Generosity*, *The Family Spirit*, and *In Praise of Goodness*, ten "mini-books" written by Mother Angelica and published by Our Lady of the Angels Monastery in the 1970s. Each section of this book corresponds to one of Mother's original mini-books. Taken together, they form a unique and beautiful work of spiritual wisdom and prayerful reverence.

Mother Angelica wrote these words on a pad of paper while in Adoration of the Blessed Sacrament in the chapel of her monastery in Irondale, Alabama. Her order, the Poor Clares of Perpetual Adoration, has been dedicated to the Blessed Sacrament since its founding, and so it is only fitting that Mother's written works were completed in His Presence.

By the mid-1970s, the Nuns of Our Lady of the Angels Monastery were printing as many as twenty-five thousand copies of these mini-books and others per day. This was truly a nascent mass-media operation, one that would lead to the creation of EWTN—the Eternal Word Television Network.

This book is a faithful representation of Mother Angelica's original work, with only the most basic corrections of printing errors, adjustments to formatting, and so on. You can be confident that you are reading an authentic presentation of the wisdom and spirituality of one of the most important figures in the history of Catholicism in America.

LIVING PRAYER

LIVING PRAYER

Seeking God

Our whole being reaches out and seeks its Creator. We want to see God and touch God. Our soul cries out, "Where are You, Lord?" and then, as the silence closes its arms around us, we hope that someday we shall hear His Voice say, "Here I am."

Will the sound of that Voice, and the touch of that Hand, be reserved for Heaven? Shall we wander as through "a trackless waste" ever seeking, but never finding? No, God manifests Himself to each one of us in various ways, in strange places, and diverse times.

He hovers over us as a "mother hen her chicks" (Matt. 23:37), listening for the sound of our voice and the cries of our heart, torn open by the thorns of sin and healed by repentant love.

As we seek Him, He is there to be found. As we cry out in supplication, He is there to listen. As we reach up to touch the hem of His garment, throughout creation, He seems to stand still and take our hand in His.

He is everywhere but our spirit must seek Him out. We cannot see Him with eyes that can see only visible creation. It is with the eyes of the soul — that intuitive vision in faith — that we see and touch God.

God is Spirit, and the mental faculties He has given us must be used to plumb the depths of the invisible reality in this life. Like a microscope that reveals tiny creatures in a drop of pond water, creatures unseen by our physical eyes, our soul must see its Creator spirit to Spirit.

Our Memory recalls the truth of His Invisible Presence, our Imagination visualizes it, our Understanding accepts it, and our Will grasps and holds it fast. That Eternal Presence, unseen by those who have eyes only for the things of this world, is ours to have and to hold.

Once we realize that prayer is Someone and not something, communion not communication, dialogue not monologue, and lastly, a union of hearts more than minds, we shall possess a sense of fulfillment, a sense of purpose, and a sense of humble dignity. We shall know for certain that we are loved by a great God.

In the Gospel of St. John, Jesus says, "Anybody who loves Me will be loved by My Father, and I shall love him and show Myself to him" (John 14:21).

Jesus manifests Himself to every soul that loves Him. That very love, deep in the center of the soul, always aglow and thirsting for the "fountain of living water" (Jer. 17:13) is proof in itself of the Divine Presence.

Living in the Present Moment

The Past and Future

God has given each one of us a gift greater than a thousand IBM machines. It is called a Memory, and everything that passes through our five senses is stored in this faculty.

We can recall the odor of a fried steak smothered with onions, and our mouths water. The remembrance of a beautiful sunrise can thrill our hearts on a sleepless night. The touch of a friend during a crisis can make us thank God for those He sends us when we are in need. The sound of a beautiful song that enraptured our souls last year can come to mind and repeat itself like a broken record, over and over.

Everything we read is stored in our memory even though our recall may not bring to mind the information we desire.

Many Christians are tortured by this faculty — tortured because of the guilt of past sins, resentments over old injuries, regrets over past omissions.

The memory of past failures can be of great benefit in the present moment if used properly. St. Paul never forgot how he persecuted the first Christians and that memory made him humble under trials and understanding during persecution (Acts 22:4-5).

Paul had many painful memories for he never forgot the numerous perils he endured for the sake of the Good News (2 Cor. 11:20-29). Neither did he forget that when he was in prison no one visited him for fear of the Jews (2 Tim. 4:16).

The problems that arise from our past are not the remembrance of that past but a need for healing — a change — a transformation by which we can put on the "mind of Christ" (1 Cor. 2:16).

We are not asked by Jesus to develop a kind of spiritual amnesia — a blocking out of everything painful. We are asked, however, to trust Him so our sins can be swallowed up in the ocean of His mercy. We are asked to develop a spirit of compassion so we can look at any person or incident in our past through His merciful Eyes.

We are asked to transform our memory through the power of His grace, to sweep it clean of all cobwebs, dirt, and superfluities that keep that faculty so cluttered up that there is no room for God.

There are three rooms in the Temple of our souls — Memory, Intellect, and Will — all three are to be returned to God adorned with the jewels of Faith, Hope, and Love.

The wooden structures given us at Baptism must be rebuilt into those solid materials fit for a King to dwell in. If we permit the original structure to deteriorate and fall into ruin by laziness and lack of zeal, we shall live in those ruins for all Eternity.

Our memories are our own, and we cannot blame anything or anyone in the past for any pain dwelling there. If we open the door to them or keep hashing over past incidents in our minds, we have only ourselves to blame.

Our lack of forgiveness makes us hate, and our lack of compassion makes us hard-hearted. Pride in our hearts makes us resentful and keeps our memory in a constant whirlwind of passion and self-pity.

From the Agony in the Garden to His death, it is consoling to see Jesus emptying His human faculties of Himself. He gave His Will to the Father completely when He said, "Thy Will be done" (Luke 22:42). He emptied His memory when He said, "Father, forgive them, for they do not know what they do" (Luke 23:34). Like the Father, He was full of compassion and mercy, and He would not permit the least resentment to enter His memory.

Like Jesus, every human being has enough memories in his past to occupy his time and thoughts continually.

There are numerous disappointments, heartaches, tragedies, misunderstandings, and separations to work untold harm upon our lives and personalities. It is not the remembrance of these incidents but the *reliving* of them that creates havoc in our souls.

Our memory can recall a painful incident so vividly that it is seen and experienced all over again. It is not only relived but exaggerated out of all proportion to truth, and as a result our emotions are aroused to such a degree that forgiveness and mercy are impossible.

We see an example of this in the life of King Saul. He never forgot the triumphant cry of the crowds, "Saul slew his thousands and David his ten thousands" (1 Sam. 18:7). The fire of jealousy was fed as Saul relived that moment over and over again. It was not long before jealousy was replaced by hatred and a desire for murder.

The *feeling* of jealousy was not the cause of Saul's fall. If he had asked God's forgiveness every time he felt this inclination, if he had praised God whose strength gave David the courage to kill Goliath, he would have been pleasing to God and never lost His favor. Eventually Saul's memory would have rid itself of self-pity, anger, and hatred. Instead, it was constantly fed and nourished by these things until he became a manic depressive. He lived in his jealousy, and his life became what his thoughts were—uncontrolled, sad, and full of hatred.

This is true of every human passion, and one day Jesus was to tell the Apostles that it was from men's hearts that evil inclinations arose, "fornication, theft, murder, adultery, avarice, malice, deceit, indecency, envy, slander, pride and folly" (Mark 7:21-23). Our hearts, created to love what is good, begin to love evil.

The frequent and sometimes constant rehearsing of past events can spark these evils mentioned by Jesus and move the Will to accomplish such acts.

We can acquire bad habits of daydreaming and live in a world of fantasy but a world nonetheless that has the power to change our personalities and create within our souls passions and hatreds that may have eternal consequences.

We are often the cause of our own misery and unhappiness, and we run from place to place looking for relief and find none. In our effort to acquire peace of mind we do not see the real cause of our uneasiness—a lack of compassion and humility.

We know that certain sins of the past create guilt complexes. Remembrances of past offenses create anger, which we cling to in spite of ourselves. We are unwilling to let go, and we do this in the name of truth.

We look at a past situation from our own point of view and justify our anger or even hatred by saying that the incident was literally unjust and uncalled for. We permit the truth of the matter to be used as a means of justifying our reactions and exercising our sinful attitudes. We very neatly create burdens and impose those burdens upon our own shoulders—carrying them around for all men to see.

Self-imposed burdens are the most difficult to release. Perhaps there is some satisfaction in reliving past situations, be they ever so painful. It makes our unkindness or hatred so justified that we feel justice is being served by the uncontrolled passions ever welling up in our hearts.

We can become so blind that we plead with God to lift this cross from our shoulders, while we unhesitatingly press it ever nearer to our hearts. We cannot see that we are to blame for our agonies. We have only to let the bitter past drop, like the superfluous baggage it is, in order to find the peace we pray for with such fervor.

Honesty is beyond our reach when we cling to resentments. Only through the compassion and mercy of our Father can our Memory be healed of all the bitterness stored within it.

If our souls are guilt laden, we will keep bringing back the cause of that guilt until it overpowers us.

Guilt feelings come from a lack of self-forgiveness. We ask God to forgive us many times when our faith triumphs, and then we have the assurance of His mercy. However, this forgiveness is somehow outside of us and like our concept of God — it is way up in the sky.

We become more and more conscious of our capacity for evil. Our repentance has only gone halfway. We have not forgiven ourselves. Our pride cannot accept the fact that we actually did such a thing.

Humility assures us that we are capable of greater evils than we have committed, and the realization of God's forgiveness increases our love. Our surprise should not be that we committed a sin but that we did not do worse.

We must realize that the God we asked forgiveness from is living in our souls, and no matter what consequence follows our mistakes, He will forgive and turn it to our good. We can trust Him and realize that He lovingly forgives us and wants us to give Him the joy of living in His Mercy.

Unfortunately, most of us nourish our guilt and waste many precious moments in self-pity and regret for what might have been.

Instead of repeating the question "Why did I do that?" we should rather ask, "What can I do now to change?" In the time it takes to utter a word—that word is already in the past. We cannot bring our past back to change it, but we can use it for our good by increasing in humility. The very remembrance of our sin can form a part of our purification.

Time is so short that as each succeeding moment follows another; we cannot miss one single opportunity for a fresh start.

We long for another chance in life—a new start, and yet as we continue living in the past, we have missed and wasted the very thing we long for—a new beginning.

Every moment of life is like a clean white sheet of paper on which we can write a new love song to God. It does not matter what tune we sang a moment ago—sorrowful or plaintive—in this new fresh moment we can change the melody to one of joyful hope or repentant love.

We must use the past to serve our present moment. We must have the self-control that permits us to utilize both the failures and successes of the past, to make this present moment more fruitful and pleasing to God.

In time of temptation, the recollection of a past fall can give us the courage to stay clear of those occasions that lead us to sin. The remembrance of God's merciful love after we have offended Him can spur our hearts on to greater love and sacrifice for His Glory.

Our present needs can often be judged by the recollection of past requirements and so help us to make more prudent decisions.

God's word must also be brought forth to give us courage in time of trial, fortitude in time of pain, gratitude in time of joy, and light in time of decision.

Most of us, however, do not find difficulty in putting some of our past to good use. The problem is the remembrance of real or imagined insults, injustices, prejudices, evil motives, personal offenses, and the ill-will of friends. These hurts find deep roots in our memory and loom before us as phantoms in the night—shadows that create fears and hatreds.

There are regrets too, that cloud our lives. We look back and see all the decisions and paths we might have chosen but did not. We dream of what might have been and then begin to feel inferior, dull, and unsuccessful.

Without mercy and compassion we cannot love ourselves or endure the failures we have caused. Since our memories have no compassion or mercy for the weaknesses of others, we have little for ourselves.

The commandment to love our neighbor as ourselves will be difficult if not impossible if our past makes us hate ourselves. The constant remembrance of past failures can destroy self-confidence and make our lives a veritable hell.

There is nothing more destructive to the soul than harboring resentments against our neighbor. It is a rebellion against the commandment to love our neighbor in the same way Jesus loves us (John 13:34-35). To deliberately permit any memory of past offenses to interfere with that commandment is to commit spiritual suicide.

Jesus told us to love our enemies; that is, we must wish them well. We must look at them with compassion and forgiveness so that the passions of revenge and hate may never enter into our memory. It is for our sake that Jesus has given us this commandment. Throughout His life we see Him treating His enemies with love. Even His reprimands were given to enlighten them that they might see the truth and accept it.

It is not easy to love our enemies or even those acquaintances whose temperaments grind on our nerves. We must remember, however, that Jesus never promised us an easy road. He told us we can expect persecution, misunderstanding, and hatred. Yes, we are to expect these evils but never succumb to them.

Unfortunately, so many of us become the very thing we hate. If our memory keeps bringing back past offenses, we become irritable and angry. If guilt plagues us, we either become defensive or develop an inferiority complex mixed with scruples. When we remember some person who caused us pain, we can become bitter and act bitter in return, for bitterness begets bitterness. So it is with every other evil.

Perhaps this is why Jesus said these evils came from the heart—we fondle them and caress them until we become what they are—evil. However, we never blame ourselves for this condition of soul. We place the blame for our misery on the one who offended us or the failure that humiliated us. Then we become a captive in our own trap. We demand to be released, but in our frenzy we fail to see the trap is locked on the inside. We have only to turn the key of compassion and mercy to be freed.

We see in both Peter and Paul a continued effort towards forgetting or using their past failures as part of their sanctification. Both men had much to forget and overcome. Their past was never permitted to take possession of their present moment.

The grace of Jesus and the power of His Spirit were strong enough to make them rise above their miseries and weaknesses. When the trials of their missions brought out those weaknesses again, they humbled themselves and praised the mercy of God, who chose weak men to confound the strong.

Paul told the Philippians, "All I can say is that I forget the past and I strain for what is still to come" (Phil. 3:13-14). He realized that he could not rest on past laurels or grieve over past sins. He was forced by the onslaughts of his explosive temperament to press forward to what was at hand and not look back at the past.

Peter too, realized how important it was to keep his memories filled with the Word of God and His goodness. In his second Epistle, Peter mentions all three faculties of the soul with particular emphasis on the memory. After exhorting the first Christians to practice the virtues of Jesus, He told them that it was necessary to "continually recall the same truths even though you already know them, and firmly hold them. I am sure it is my duty, as long as I am in this tent, to keep stirring you up with reminders" (2 Peter 1:12, 14).

Their Intellects comprehended the truth so they *knew* what was expected of them. Their Wills were strong, and they followed Jesus, "they held truth firm." But Peter realized that if these first Christians were to persevere, they must continually bring to their minds through their memories the recollection of Jesus, His revelations, and His Love.

Not satisfied with just giving his converts many reminders, Peter reassured them by saying, "I shall take great care that after my own departure you will still have a means to recall these things to memory" (2 Peter 1:15).

Scripture makes it clear that every human being has something in his past that he is either ashamed of or regrets. It also tells us of God's mercy and the good we can derive from past failures. We must work together with God to bring good out of all our mistakes.

Jesus Himself used the suffering caused by the malice, ambition, and hatred of evil men to redeem us. Jesus, too, had to keep His memory full of the Father's compassion. He never permitted the remembrance of being born in a cold cave or the hatred of Herod deter Him from showing mercy to sinners or giving health to the sick. The more coldness He received from men, the more love He gave. The more offenses He suffered, the more mercy He extended.

Our memory is a precious gift from God. Created in the image of the Father, it must grow in that image and become as compassionate and merciful as He is.

We must use our memory for whatever the present moment requires but have the power to lay it to rest when it begins to disturb our peace and create within us a hardness of heart.

Linked with our memory is another faculty—Imagination —that can also create havoc if it has free rein. We can project the future in such vivid pictures that we suffer pain and emotional upheaval. The fear of sickness can be projected for a long excruciating period of time, and death looms before us as a traumatic experience.

The fear of risks also causes our imagination to foresee great failure and humiliation when we are faced with a decision. We can actually live through some future event with tears, fears, and despair.

We foresee doom on the horizon, and our intellect and will become paralyzed from the vivid picture presented by our imagination. Each one of us can recall various times and places where this faculty was permitted to run wild and place our souls in a state of confusion and sadness.

This faculty not only embellishes past events and projects future ones; it can also make the present moment difficult to endure. Left unchecked, it can create negative attitudes so strong that lies become truth and truth distorted.

Our imagination was not given to us to be used as an instrument of torture. It is not to create fears and doubts in God and ourselves. It is not to trigger our emotions to the brink of despair, but it can and does do all these things when it is uncontrolled.

Whatever painful event our memory brings to mind, our imagination can embellish and exaggerate beyond all bounds of reason. These self-imposed burdens can make life an endurance test designed to crush our spirits. We cry out to God for help and then become more embittered when no help is in sight. We forget, however, that we already have the solution to our plight.

Jesus gave us an example of how to live under every possible situation. He asked us to pray for our enemies so hatred would never take hold of us, but we seem to think that the person who offended us is different and somehow does not fit into the category of those for whom we should pray.

He exhorted us not to worry about tomorrow, but we think our tomorrow is different, and we rationalize our concern and fears. We do not trust Him, and the precept to seek first the kingdom, becomes the dream of an idealist.

He asked us to be compassionate and merciful but we feel our self-respect would be in jeopardy if we were not frank, cautious, and prudent.

He told us to be meek and humble of heart, but this too does not seem to fit into our concept of human dignity. Our pride rebels against truth. We will accept insult, importunity, and rudeness to keep our jobs, but we will not do it for Jesus.

Mental discipline is beyond our reach when we become attached to our opinions, fears, resentments, prejudices, and guilt. We are for the most part Christians who speak much, perform little, complain a great deal, and change slightly.

In imitation of the first Christians we must set our goals ever higher and never rest satisfied with our progress. We must possess a serene urgency in regard to holiness of life — a realization that God may call us at any moment, any split second of time, and we must be at our best. Years are spent preparing ourselves for a tiny moment when our souls will leave our bodies.

In this context, it is important that we look at our present moment because in one of them God will say, "Come."

Our entire life will be represented in that moment. The way we used pain, suffering, and disappointments will be manifested by our degree of union with His will at that precious moment. Resentments that we have harbored and cherished will be there to shame us. The virtues we have practiced — the fruit He bore in us — will be as many jewels in our Wedding Garment. Yes, every moment of life is like a new creation, a new chance, a fresh opportunity, a time of renewal, and someday, the springboard to Eternity.

The Present Moment

It would seem easy to live in the present moment. It is obvious to those around us that we lose our peace at the slightest remembrance of a painful past and are disheartened by a glimpse of the future.

The whole life of Jesus is an example of living in the present moment, and although He looked forward to His Passion — a future event in His life — He never permitted that foreknowledge to influence His present moment.

He knew Judas would betray Him. That knowledge did not prevent Jesus from giving Judas the power to heal on that memorable day He sent out His Apostles to preach the Good News.

Jesus asked us all to live in the present moment when He said, "Do not worry about your life and what you eat, nor about your body and how you are to clothe it" (Matt. 6:25-34). This is a preoccupation with what is to come, and to impress upon our minds His true meaning, Jesus used two things that are absolutely necessary for daily living — eating and clothing.

"Surely," He says, "life means more than food and the body more than clothing." Here He tries to impress upon us that what happens to our body and soul is so much more important than those things outside of it. The word "worry" that Jesus used so often in this admonition is typical of "living" in past or future events.

Jesus did not say we should not supply those needs both for ourselves and others. He admonished us not to worry about them, not to "live" in these necessities, not to permit exterior things to control our minds and hearts.

He called those who worry "men of little faith"—pagans who set their hearts on "things" and not the kingdom. The heart of the disciple of Jesus was to be free to love Him in the present moment because His Father in Heaven knew what he needed and would take care.

"Set your hearts on His kingdom first, and on His righteousness, and all these other things will be given you as well" (Matt. 6:33). This is a call to set our minds and hearts to doing His will as He presents it to us in the present moment. We are to look at Him as He takes on various disguises and be holy as He is holy.

The future—which is tomorrow—is not to be our care. "Do not worry about tomorrow; tomorrow will take care of itself. Each day has enough trouble of its own" (Matt. 6:34). We are asked by Jesus to be concerned with whatever this day, this present moment, brings to us. He reminds us that there is enough trouble in this moment to occupy our minds and try our souls. He does not want us to add the burden of tomorrow to the concerns of today. God bestows specific aids called "actual grace" to each succeeding moment. Each grace is measured to help us be like Jesus in the present moment. We do not possess the grace to endure the pains of cancer at a time when we only need grace to endure a headache.

We must understand that God does not distribute His specific graces before they are needed. Our Baptism and the following of His commandments keeps us in a state of grace, but every moment of our lives God bestows those special actual graces that are to help us be like Jesus.

Like Mary, we need to be "full of grace" so when God requests some sacrifice of us, as He did her, we shall cooperate with the grace of the moment with all our heart.

One of the petitions of the Our Father is "Give us this our daily bread." This daily bread is not a twenty-four-hour span. It is the grace of the moment and the material needs of that moment. It is a minute by minute, day by day request. We are children of a bountiful Father, heirs to a kingdom, so we are to ask the Father to supply our needs. Our trust, however, must be one of childlike confidence in His Providence. It is in that spirit that we realize everything that happens to us has first passed through His hands and His grace is with us.

St. Paul received a surprise answer from Jesus when he asked to be delivered from his affliction. "My grace is sufficient for you" (2 Cor. 12:9). When Paul thought he had reached the end of his rope, Jesus reminded him to forget the past and live in the present moment—that is where the grace was hidden. Paul possessed all he needed to overcome. It was when he bereaved his past and projected future sufferings that life became intolerable. He missed the grace of the moment that God was extending to him by losing hope and courage.

Even the parable of the mustard seed can be related to the present moment. Our life is made up of millions of mustard seeds—millions of moments. The faithful gardening of these seeds will one day result in a rich harvest.

Jesus laid down a condition of following Him. He said, "If anyone wants to be a follower of mine, let him renounce himself and take up his cross every day and follow me" (Luke 9:24). We must follow Jesus by renouncing ourselves—putting ourselves aside — emptying ourselves moment to moment — day by day.

This is such a gigantic task that to project a lifetime of self-denial would present unsurmountable difficulties. Discouragement would fill our souls to the brim, and our weaknesses would overwhelm us.

We may find it hard to be virtuous for a lifetime, but everyone can be virtuous for a moment — a moment at a time. Is this perhaps the "narrow gate" Jesus spoke of to His disciples (Matt. 7:13)? How many are there who have the confidence to trust their past to His mercy and their future to His Providence? How many are there who possess enough mental discipline to use past and future to their advantage and then forget them to peacefully pursue the duties of the present moment?

The present moment — the *now* — is like a sacrament, for a sacrament is a visible sign of an invisible reality. Whatever is happening to us in our moment to moment existence is a visible manifestation of God's action in our lives. It is an opportunity to grow in grace — in the image of Jesus. God speaks to each one of us in the present moment, and He calls each of us to union with Himself. His wisdom provides what we need in order to change and be transformed into another Christ.

Our difficulty in seeing God in the present moment usually stems from the realization that we are often the victims of the failures, weaknesses, evil, and bad intentions of our neighbor. We find it near impossible to see Jesus in these kinds of situations. God is love, He is good, and He is merciful. We cannot equate a tragic or difficult situation with His Attributes.

Perhaps this is our mistake. We must realize that God does not cause evil but He does *permit* it. Jesus told us that the world would hate us but we were not to worry because He overcame it (John 16:33).

His resurrection proved His assertion that He would overcome, but it is noteworthy to realize He permitted men to do anything they pleased to Him. The Father did not intervene and stop it all in the name of justice. He let His sinless Son suffer at the hands of the sinners He came to save.

We are reminded by Jesus that the servant is not above the master and although we are not called upon to make the sacrifices He did, we are expected to live as children of light — not darkness.

He wants us to be like Him and see the Father's guiding hand every moment of our daily lives. To do this we must be free of the burden of past regrets, resentments, successes, and failures. We must also be free of the fears of what the future will bring.

This means having a clear mind for the duties of the present moment. It means to be at home in our souls—to possess the self-control so necessary for prayer and a life of union with God.

Jesus has asked us to pray without ceasing. We cannot say prayers without ceasing but we can make our life a living prayer—a preparation for that time of day when we speak to God and tell Him of our Love.

To be in love with God is to love Him with our whole heart, mind, soul, and strength. It is to relate everything in our lives to Him—to see Him—to love Him—to serve Him and to live for Him. It is to be aware of His Presence, His Love, His Mercy and Existence. It is to have joy in the midst of sorrow and self-control in times of temptation. It is to empty ourselves of all selfishness and constantly be filled with the grace of His Spirit. It is to think like Jesus, be like Jesus, and love like Jesus. It is never to leave Him alone in our souls while we run after the trinkets of this world.

Is it possible to live a life of holiness in this world? Has Jesus demanded the impossible? To answer these questions we must look back to the converts of Peter, Paul, and the other

Apostles. These converts were called "Christians"—followers of Jesus.

We must see how these first Christians used every moment of their lives to change themselves into images of Jesus. When they were not talking to Jesus in prayer, their lives manifested the virtues of Jesus.

They did not permit themselves the self-indulgence of living in the past or future. They never knew when their new-found Faith would demand the sacrifice of home, land, and life. They were determined to live every moment of their lives for and with Jesus.

They failed as we all do, but when they did, they rose up from those failures with courage and love. This is *not to say* that they were perfect and modern-day Christians are not; *it is only to say* how they lived in their present moment amidst great trials and difficulties, in the hopes that we may regain what we may have lost and begin anew to live a life of fervor as they did.

Perhaps by looking at them we may observe how they prayed without ceasing in their hearts, minds, and souls.

The Presence of Jesus in their souls was a glorious experience to the first Christians. It was not always a "feeling" experience, but it was a constant, continuous Faith experience — an awareness of God dwelling in their souls, and in their neighbor. The painful circumstances of life were merely opportunities for them to find their Lord, and to rejoice that they were counted worthy to suffer for His Name's sake (Acts 5:41).

Throughout the Epistles and Acts, we find these first Christians imbued with a spirit of awareness and mission — awareness of God's Presence within them and a realization that they were to manifest that Presence to their neighbor.

To do this, they had to pray — to commune with the Master constantly. Their whole being was to change into something wonderful — into a son of God. Every day was a challenge — every day an opportunity to grow into the Image they loved so much.

The question in the minds of Christians today is: "How did they do it?" It is obvious, from the heroic deeds they accomplished, the pain they suffered, and the martyrdom they endured, that they had something we lack.

- They had the Spirit — but so do we.
- They had the Eucharist — but so do we.
- They had men who taught them the Word of God — but so do we.

34

- ☞ They had communal worship—but so do we.
- ☞ They prayed without ceasing—*but we do not.*
- ☞ They possessed a faith vision—but we do not.

They began in their prayer life where most of us end. They had no degrees of prayer to attain, no definitions to guide them, no steps to follow. They never knew the difference between vocal prayer and the prayer of union. They seemed to have little knowledge of ways and means, but they had a great experience with God as Father.

They had a simple humility that acknowledged their sins, and reached out to Jesus as Lord and Savior. They buried themselves, their personalities, their possessions, goals, and desires —buried them in Jesus. Looking at themselves with honesty, they cried out, "Abba, Father."

It would be centuries before men could define what these first Christians possessed. It would take centuries more to explain the intricacies of a life of prayer and union with God. But to these first fruits of Redemption, life was a challenge and a continuous prayer—a goal that love would attain and perseverance acquire.

They had only one desire and that was to be like Jesus in their everyday life. They arrived at this goal through the power and grace of the Holy Spirit and persevering effort in attaining the Prayer of Imitation.

This was the Good News to be proclaimed to the world. They were called to be like Jesus and thereby prove that Jesus was Lord.

We will look at the way they kept Jesus in their hearts and minds, and grew in grace moment to moment.

Prayer of Imitation

Throughout all the Epistles and the Acts, one gets the impression that the first Christians ate, drank, slept, talked, and argued about nothing else but their beliefs and their Jesus. When they became engrossed in the affairs of the world and returned to their old ways, the Sacred Writers reproved them severely.

They were called upon to work for a living and be hospitable (Rom. 12:13). Most of all, they were to be imitators of their Divine Model and count it a blessing to suffer for His Name.

The words of Jesus were not merely the foundation of their faith but the maxims by which they lived. His words found a home in their hearts. That home was a place in which their spirits grew into the likeness of Jesus.

They were careful that the house was swept clean of the dirt of sin and the dust of selfishness. It was not filled with the cluttering superfluities that make it impossible to move about with ease.

They began their Imitation of Jesus by emptying themselves of all the excess baggage that burdened them.

It wasn't their material possessions that weighed them down, because they shared everything they had with one another. It must be noted that they wanted for nothing. In sharing, they were not deprived, and when some of the widows of the Hellenists were overlooked, a complaint was made for a fairer distribution (Acts 4:34, 6:1-6).

These first Christians realized that inner burdens and attachments were the real possessions that must be relinquished for the good of the Kingdom and their own holiness. Their new lives were centered upon the goal of emptying themselves and being filled with God.

"Free your minds, then, of encumbrances," St. Peter told them, "control them and put your trust in nothing but the grace that will be given you.... You must be scrupulously careful as long as you are living away from your home" (1 Pet. 1:13, 17).

Their real home was Heaven, so this world and everything in it took on the appearance of a temporary residence — a place away from home — an Inn on a journey. With this concept in mind and the Divine Promises in their hearts, they became pilgrims and travelers who were on a journey.

Like all journeys, it took on the aspect of a challenge and an adventure. They vied with one another, not in worldly pursuits, but in the Imitation of Jesus.

"I urge you, my dear people," St. Peter exhorted them, "while you are visitors and pilgrims, to keep yourselves free from selfish passions that attack the soul" (1 Pet. 2:11).

Life began to have meaning as they listened to Paul say, "recognizing that they (the prophets of old) were only strangers and nomads on earth ... they made it quite plain that they were in search of their real homeland.... They were longing for a better homeland, their heavenly homeland" (Heb. 11:13-14).

The sudden realization that this world was not "home" gave the Christians a whole new kind of life and way of living. They not only realized this truth but were told where "home" was and how to prepare for it.

They did not have the struggle for detachment that we have because in the realization that earth was not home, everything they clung to suddenly seemed unimportant.

This detachment did not make them indifferent. No, they worked, and worked hard, were concerned about others and shared what they possessed with them. They lived a full life but were never constrained or tied down by what they accomplished or the demands life made on them.

They were free, and that freedom was paid for by the Precious Blood of Jesus (1 Pet. 1:18-19). Jesus told them, "If you make My Word your home, you will indeed be My disciples; you will learn the truth, and the truth will make you free" (John 8:32).

The truth that God lived in these souls through the power of His Spirit, and Heaven was their true home, made these people new men and women. Their minds thought in a new way; their actions were Christ-like; their motives pure; their souls clothed in a faith that moved the mountains of evil around them.

Their whole lives suddenly had a purpose and a mission. They saw God everywhere and in everything that happened to them. Most of all they now had Someone to follow—a perfect Model by whom to measure themselves.

Though the Gospels had not been written, each Christian would write down those words of Jesus that appealed to him, memorize them, and then live by them. And Peter and Paul began to write letters that explained the Faith. These letters were copied and passed around as precious treasures.

Jesus had told them that they should dance for joy when they were persecuted because their reward was great in Heaven (Matt. 5:11-12).

That one statement gave meaning to their lives. For centuries the world experienced pain and suffering without meaning or purpose. Human life was expendable, and compassion was considered a weakness. Sickness and injustice were everywhere, and the law of the land was to survive no matter what the cost.

All pagans came from darkness, lived in darkness, and when they died, the blackest of nights awaited them. The only happiness available was the pleasures of this world, and one grabbed as much as he could, for tomorrow he died and there was nothing to come.

When a pagan looked at Israel for hope, he found a semblance of inner peace. However, the Chosen People argued among themselves as to what was to come. Some believed in an afterlife; some did not. To the pagan looking for solutions to his doubts, this was little comfort. No one seemed to have answers to his doubts and questions.

And then a Light pierced the darkness, and although it, too, created a darkness by virtue of its intensity, this new darkness was the kind mixed with awesome mystery, not doubt. It was a darkness that gave direction and peace and assurance, for now the believers held a Hand, and that Hand was God's. They now experienced a Presence, and that Presence was His Spirit in their souls. Yes, life itself and the world they lived in didn't change too much, but each one of them changed, and they would eventually change the world.

They would meet together, sometimes in secret, to speak of Jesus. Each one would tell of his experiences, or of some words given him by the Apostles, and all would pray and sing psalms. They would share in His Body and Blood at the Breaking of Bread and go out into the world to put into practice what they had learned.

Never before did they have a God to imitate. All the gods they had as pagans were far above them and struck fear into their hearts. The God of Israel, too, was an awesome God, whose very name many would not pronounce. How could one imitate a God so far above one's own nature, perfect and holy in everything He did?

And then came Jesus — Man and God. He was Someone they could relate to, Someone they could follow, Someone who experienced their misery and triumphed, Someone who overcame the darkness and showed them the Great Light.

They changed course in their journey of life. They left the directionless desert for a road often rocky and mountainous, but nonetheless a road with a definite direction and an end in view.

Time became the distance between where they were and where they were to go. Jesus became the Way to their destination, and Heaven was their Homeland.

In this context, everything was seen in the light of Eternity. Every action was judged by the light of Jesus. Every moment of time was an opportunity to grow in His Image and advance closer to the Kingdom. Everything took on a new look, every life situation a new meaning. Every human being was an image of God and every suffering an opportunity to be like Jesus.

Their lives had a purpose as God guided them every step of the way. They soon realized that if they were to persevere on their journey, keep following His Way, and stay on the "straight and narrow path," they needed spiritual energy.

They needed a constant source of strength, and they found that source in prayer.

To the first Christians prayer was like breathing; it was part of their moment to moment existence. It was not a tedious obligation but an outpouring of the heart to Someone very close — Someone living in their very souls.

Their prayer was a desire to be like Jesus, and they did not separate their lives from prayer. Prayer became such a part of life that it was woven throughout it like golden threads in a tapestry.

To think of Jesus was to pray. To love Jesus was to pray. To talk of Jesus was to pray. And to be like Jesus was to glorify the Father.

Jesus told them, "It is to the glory of My Father that you should bear fruit, and then you will be My disciples" (John 15:8). To give glory to the Father was to them the highest form of prayer. To be a disciple was the best way to show their gratitude for Redemption.

These Christians studied the life of Jesus and saw what He did and how He acted under every circumstance. They realized that "because He Himself had been through temptations, He was able to help others who were tempted" (Heb. 2:18).

"That is why," St. Paul told them, "all you who are holy brothers and have had the same heavenly call, should turn your minds to Jesus" (Heb. 3:1). This was the secret of their ability to pray without ceasing. In everything they did, they turned their minds to Jesus.

They were to "keep their minds constantly occupied in doing good works" because they were now sons of God and brothers of Jesus (Titus 3:8).

"You see," St. Paul reminded them, "God's grace has been revealed ... and taught us that what we have to do is to give up everything that does not lead us to God, and all our worldly ambitions; we must be self-restrained, and live good and religious lives in this present world" (Titus 2:11-12).

They had to give up their old ways and adopt new ones. The realization of Heaven as Homeland detached them from their possessions and the realization that the Father sent His Son to redeem them, detached them from themselves. They thought of nothing but the new life and put off the old like a torn garment.

The words of Paul ran through their minds over and over, "For anyone who is in Christ, there is a new creation; the old creation has gone, and now the new one is here" (2 Cor. 5:17).

"We groan as we wait with longing to put on our Heavenly Home" (2 Cor. 5:2).

These two thoughts gave them wings to fly into the arms of God. No longer fearful of the future, no longer burdened with their past, they lived the present moment like Jesus, their Model and Lord.

They were "Ambassadors of Christ," His "letter to the world," sons of the Father, and witnesses that Jesus was Lord. They belonged to God and proved they were sons "by great fortitude in times of suffering, hardship, and distress, by purity, knowledge, patience, kindness, a spirit of holiness, a love free of affectation, by being prepared for honor or disgrace, blame or praise" (2 Cor. 6:4-8).

They combined all these goals into one goal—to be like Jesus. All the power of their Wills was geared in one direction—to be like Jesus. They had only one desire, and only one ambition—to be like Jesus.

- They would be humble, because He told them to learn from Him, for He was meek and humble of Heart.
- They would not worry, because He told them to trust the Father, who cared for them.

- ☞ They would leave their burdens to God, because He told them not to judge.

- ☞ They would look for the invisible reality behind life's sufferings, because He gave them Beatitudes to ensure their joy.

- ☞ They would never feel lonely, because He told them the Spirit would live in them and bring to their minds His Words.

- ☞ They would share with one another and make hospitality their special boast because He told them to love one another as He loved them.

They knew in the depths of their souls that for some mysterious reason God loved them with a tremendous love and they had to return that love in the best way possible.

"You were darkness once," Paul told them, "but now you are light in the Lord; be like children of light, for the effects of the light are seen in complete goodness and right living and truth" (Eph. 5:8-9).

The power of His death and Resurrection made children of darkness into beacons of light. The power of His Spirit changed their lives and made them radiate goodness. Their mission was to "expose darkness by contrast" (Eph. 5:11).

They did not need to preach Jesus—they *were* Jesus. They took upon themselves His beautiful qualities, enhanced their own personalities by modeling them on His, and then led others to the Father by their Joy and Love.

They were told to "imitate God and follow Christ by loving as He loved" (Eph. 5:1), and that imitation constituted a prayer style that was before unknown.

Their prayer life before was one of fearsome homage. The words they spoke were measured and reverent, mixed with a feeling of inferiority and inadequacy.

Now they knew Jesus, God's own Son. They possessed His very Spirit; they were heirs with Him of an eternal life, and this realization made their whole lives a Prayer of Imitation.

In everything they said or did, the words of Paul renewed their determination to be like Jesus. "Do not model yourselves on the behavior of the world around you," he said, "but let your behavior change, modeled by your new mind." "In your minds, you must be the same as Christ Jesus" (Rom. 12:2; Phil. 2:5).

Their lives were made new by thinking like Jesus and this spiritual revolution changed their actions, their attitudes, their goals, and their desires. Their lives became a prayer, for every moment was colored by the longing to be like their God (Eph. 4:23).

Jesus said that with Him in them they would bear much fruit but without Him they could do nothing. They must have found that statement difficult to understand since every human being desires to be himself and wants his personality to be completely his own.

It must have taken them a little time to realize what it all meant. When they compared themselves to Jesus, they became more and more aware of the vast difference between themselves and Jesus.

They observed His actions under every kind of situation, heard or read his words of comfort and encouragement, and saw Him triumph over His enemies. They realized that it was not a matter of being molded into one communal pattern. It was not a matter of giving up one's personality or will; it was a matter of choosing, of using one's free will, of being humble enough to know He had something better to give, and of loving enough to want to be like Him.

It was a choice one made of drinking at the fountain of living water, of being filled with the grace that comes from God alone, and of developing one's natural good qualities into God-like actions.

It was not slavery, it was freedom—an opportunity to replace a vacuum for an emptiness that was constantly being filled—a narrowness that was continually being expanded.

Their lives were so changed that everyone recognized them as Christians. Their desires, attitudes, speech, actions, and opinions were all changed in a way that attracted pagans from every nation.

Yes, their lives were one beautiful Prayer, always changing in its expression, always harmonizing with life situations, always in tune with the melody they heard from the Heart of God.

Prayer of the Mind

The first Christians soon learned that there were many ways of expressing themselves to God. There were times they spoke to God about His Beauty—or their needs—and that was conversational Prayer.

They spoke to Him silently in their thoughts, and as they spoke to Him they realized He answered them. He answered in the same way they spoke—by thought.

Many times they were afraid as they were hunted like animals—and that very fear reached up to God for help. It was at times like these that they felt a surge of courage revive their spirits, and the words of Jesus would run through their minds. Then they wondered why they had been so afraid. They would realize God had spoken to them, and His Word was proven by power.

There were other times when they had to fight the enemy within and they realized they needed mental discipline to control the spiritual faculties that caused such havoc in their souls.

They would quiet their minds by using their memories to recall some incident in the life of Jesus. This effort calmed that faculty of any resentment that might be deposited there. To ensure their thought of Jesus taking hold, they would use their imagination to picture the scene, and suddenly it was as if they were really there. They would feel the sentiments of His Heart in that situation and begin to apply them to themselves.

To the first Christians this kind of Prayer was a "Jesus experience," but to us it is a "meditation." To them it was a heart experience; to us it is a mind experience. To them it was a faith vision resulting in a change of life; to us it is an intellectual exercise resulting in speculations and theological arguments. They prayed and changed *themselves*; we pray and change *things*.

Some worldly Christians do not live and breathe Jesus. Their prayer life is limited to conversational Prayer when in need, formal Prayer when they cannot think of what to say to God, and sometimes mental Prayer when their souls are at peace.

All these forms of Prayer are limited to a time and a place. They are part of our prayer life, but only a part, and if that life is fed only by these forms of prayer, Jesus will come and go in our lives according to our needs, spare time, and abilities. He will not be our Constant Companion and Intimate Friend. We shall never pray without ceasing.

The first Christians' Prayer of Imitation gave them the necessary drive to bring about in their mind and will the desire to be like Jesus in everything. In order to prepare their hearts for this transformation, they read and reread everything that related to Jesus and His Personality.

It was the Personality of Jesus that the Christians were trying to emulate. They realized Jesus was the perfect model of how a son of God acted and thought.

In order to perfect their own personalities and bring out those qualities that were buried by sin, weakness, and imperfections, the Christians had to keep their eyes, mind, and heart on the Divine Model. They had seen other imperfect men like Peter, Paul, James, and John develop within themselves qualities of soul that astounded the world. They seemed to be born again, to be full of joy, in control of themselves, and unhampered by the cares of this world.

They realized that the foundation of their actions was their thoughts and so they began to fill their minds with a mental concept of Jesus that wove itself into every situation and brought to their minds a pattern and parallel between themselves and Him.

Because they loved Him, this effort was never forced or strained. It was the natural consequence of a deep love—a love that made the parties involved one.

When they heard or read of Jesus "feeling sorry" for a crowd of people, they were not satisfied with thinking about the scene to contemplate His compassion; they entered into His Spirit and began to "feel" as He felt.

Had He not put His Spirit into them when they were baptized? Were they not called upon to follow Him as faithful disciples? Well then, they would cooperate with that Spirit and act accordingly.

His compassion for sinners would be theirs, and they would develop the Gifts given to them by using every situation to grow into His image.

Their minds had to "think like Jesus." Their hearts had to "feel" like Jesus. Their voices had to spread the Good News about Jesus.

St. Paul had told them in a letter to "guard your hearts and your thoughts in Christ Jesus" (Phil. 4:7). This is how they would persevere in their Prayer of Imitation — they would set a guard at the door of their Memory, careful that no bitterness or resentment ever took up residence there. They would fill their minds with "everything that was good, pure, true and noble" (Phil. 4:8).

When they were tempted to anger or to cursing, they would immediately think of Jesus as He stood before His enemies in calm serenity. Their contemplation looked beyond the "thinking" stage. Their imagination pictured Jesus in perfect self-control, and their *hearts* responded by doing the same as He did.

They used their minds to recall the life of Jesus, but they went further and penetrated into the Heart and sentiments of Jesus. Their minds not only remembered and saw what He did, but their spirits, united to His Spirit, began to "feel" as He felt and to absorb His Spirit. They literally "put on" Christ, and their lives bore the fruit of that union.

The minds and hearts of the first Christians worked together in harmony. Their faith was not the prisoner of their minds, but was made fruitful by penetrating the whole person, so that it touched every facet of life.

Faith, thoughts, and actions were as one. They guarded all three so no conflict ever came between them, trying not to *think* one thing and *do* another. With the Spirit of Christ in their souls, they had to act accordingly but could not until their thoughts were under control and their hearts totally God's.

They had to see everything that happened to them through the eyes of faith. When they were persecuted and their reason told them to go back to the old ways, Faith told them to dance for joy for their reward was great in Heaven.

They blessed their enemies and prayed for them as a remedy to cure the cancer of resentment and never permitted it entrance into their minds. Jesus gave them this secret to peace, and they followed in His footsteps.

When home, friends, and lands were lost for the sake of the Kingdom, they thought of Jesus leaving Heaven and living on earth with no place to rest His head. Entering into that spirit of sacrifice, they left all for the sake of Jesus.

Life as a Christian was often painful but it was never without a challenge, fruit, or opportunity. They stumbled and fell many times but merely used these occasions as stopping places in the journey of life—places to take stock of themselves, replenish their strength by repentance and prayer, and move forward with greater earnestness.

The Spirit of Jesus was a power within them that gave them the opportunity to choose on every occasion between being weak or strong, good or bad, holy or sinful, a son of the world or a son of God. It was a personal choice, but the power to accomplish the best thing would always be present.

If they became so absorbed in the situation or in themselves, they would fall prey to weakness, sin, and imperfections. They could not bear fruit alone. But when they *thought* like Jesus, and took upon themselves His Spirit, they bore the fruit of Jesus and acted as a son of God, not a son of the world.

It was difficult, for human nature revels in pride and recoils at humility, seeks independence and rejects obedience, desires luxury and spurns poverty, covets pleasure and rebels at penance or sacrifice. It was not possible to make such changes alone. Only God's grace could make mere men sons of God and capable of heroic virtue. They had to choose often and every day between acting like men or sons.

One thing they learned—they had to control their thoughts. Jesus told them to forgive their enemies and do good to those who cursed them. They soon realized it was for their own sake that He told them this. They noticed that every time they began to hate a persecutor, it interfered with their union with God. Their minds became cluttered with resentful and revengeful feelings. An eye for an eye, a tooth for a tooth soon made them into vessels of hate, not love.

They became irritable and critical and were thrown back to their "old ways." The newborn man seemed to die and wither and he stood alone, buffeted on every side by temptations and doubts.

Yes, when Jesus told them to forgive and have compassion on those who offended them and pray for them, it was to keep their own souls untouched by the hatred of others. They were to have pity on those who did not know Jesus and pray for them so they, too, might be born again or at least have the opportunity to make a choice between God and the enemy.

They were to shake the dust of dissension and hatred from themselves and let their peace return to them (Matt. 10:14).

Paul had to remind them often of the Lord's Will for them. "Do all you can to live at peace with everyone. Never try to get revenge; leave that, my friends, to God's anger. If your enemy is hungry, you should give him food, or if he is thirsty, drink.... Resist evil and do good" (Rom. 12:18-21). By doing this they were to win over many who lived in darkness. The enemy of God, who was Prince of this world, would lose many followers by the virtuous lives of these Christians.

"Let us not lose sight of Jesus," Paul told them over and over (Heb. 12:2). Everything the Christians were before their conversion had to change. They could no longer be spiteful, deceitful, hypocritical, envious, or critical of their neighbor (1 Pet. 2:1).

They were to agree among themselves, be sympathetic, love one another, have compassion, and be self-effacing (1 Pet. 3:8). The only way they could accomplish this was to "think of what Christ suffered in this life, and then arm themselves with the same resolution that He had" (1 Pet. 4:1).

Their minds were to be disciplined and trained to think in a new way, guided by a new set of principles and values, and motivated by a deep love for Jesus. They had to acquire a "habit" of thinking like Jesus.

Peter realized the importance of renewing their minds when he said, "I am continually recalling the same truths to you, even though you already know them and firmly hold them. I am sure it is my duty to keep stirring you up with reminders … so after my departure you still have a means to recall these things to memory" (2 Pet. 1:12-15).

He prayed that the "morning star" would rise in their minds so their lives would reflect the Light captured there and the whole world see their goodness, understanding, patience, kindness, self-control, true devotion, and love (2 Pet. 1:3-11).

Christianity was so unlike any religion of its time. It was made up of people who worshiped, prayed, and shared together. The religion or religious sects that were so numerous were only concerned with the individual and the Absolute. To fear and pacify was the essence of their worship of idols. Their relationship was never one of the heart and never reached out to their neighbor in love.

The Christians accepted invisible truth and called it Faith. They lived by these truths and called it Hope. They permitted these truths to change them and their lives and called it

Love. The total person reached up to God in love and then stretched itself out to the world in love. That was the Christian's cross—a vertical relationship with God that was so powerful, it diffused itself in all directions. This was the cross they were to carry.

This is the Cross Jesus carried: His love for His Father and mankind made Him empty Himself to the point where "He did not count equality with God a thing to be clung to" (Phil. 2:6). He emptied Himself to be obedient to His Father. By that obedience He made reparation for the sin of Adam and Eve. He opened up the gates of Heaven and merited Divine Adoption for all of us.

His humility confounded the pride of the enemy and showed us the way to Heaven. Behind both His obedience and humility was a great love—love for the Father and love for mankind.

Filled with love, He came down and took upon Himself our nature and then sent His Spirit to fill us with a Divine participation in that nature.

The first Christians realized this truth and reciprocated by loving Jesus and their neighbor with the love of the Spirit who dwelt within them. Their one desire was to give glory to the

Father as Jesus did and they would do it in the same way—by obedience, humility, and love.

They would fill their minds with the Word of God, their imagination with the life of Jesus, their understanding with Faith, and their will with love.

Christianity was, above all, *Someone*, and that fact demanded an intellectual assent to truth and a total giving of the heart to Jesus. It was a Faith that reached up to Heaven and touched God and a deep burning Love that spread out and touched each neighbor.

It was a life of choices and decisions—some right and some wrong—but each one building up some part of the soul and making it into a new creation.

The first Christians believed and loved, and they did both with joy and freedom. They would *see* Jesus in everyone and *be* Jesus to everyone.

They would imitate the whole Christ by doing everything for the Glory of the Father and seeing everything in the light of Eternity rather than time.

Most of all, they would manifest the Spirit who lived within them—the Spirit of Love.

Prayer of the Heart

The first Christians soon realized that if they were to persevere in the new life they were chosen to live, they had to love and love intensely. It was this element of love that made Christianity so different from any other religion.

Man is a being of emotion and to live only in Faith and Hope would be to live in a desert with light and air but no warmth. Man needs incentive and drive to propel him out of darkness into light, or, better still, to radiate light in the midst of darkness.

Life was difficult at best. Though Christianity gave them peace within, it created havoc around them. It made some men examine their consciences and showed them up for what they really were—false and tyrannical. It takes a great man to see himself and change, but the world was sometimes ruled by small men—men who rebelled at the sight of themselves. They struck out at these Christians with a fury that only hatred could produce.

These Christians had to keep themselves above every situation that tended to drag their souls down and make them want to retaliate at anger and hatred.

They had to nourish and maintain within themselves a never-ending source of love. They had to feed their souls with life-giving water.

Jesus had sent the Advocate to dwell in their souls, and they were determined that nothing would interfere with that union. Every moment of their lives had to be used to grow in the Image of Jesus.

Faith gave them a belief, and Hope a goal, but to keep both alive and active they needed to Love.

Faith settled the doubts in their intellects, and Hope calmed their emotions, but they needed Love to give them the endurance to persevere.

Faith told them *what* they believed, and Hope told them *why*, but it was Love that told them *Whom* they believed in.

Faith gave them *something*, and Hope gave them *some place*, but Love gave them *Someone*.

In the journey of life, Faith was the boat, Hope the anchor, and Love the rudder.

They had to maintain an ever growing Love for God and neighbor and they looked to Jesus to tell them how. One day Jesus told His Apostles, "If anyone loves Me, he will keep My word, and My Father will love him, and We shall come and make Our home with him" (John 14:23).

The secret then was to keep His word and the Trinity would live in them. The Spirit made them sons of God at Baptism; an indelible seal was placed upon them — a seal never to be erased in time or eternity. Like the sons of men, they had to grow and mature in their new life and that life was fed by God Himself.

"And My Word is not my own," Jesus said, "it is the Word of the One who sent Me" (John 14:24). Was the "Word" something they heard, or was it Someone they loved?

Somehow they knew that the words that passed through their minds and the emotions of their hearts were inseparable. They noticed when they read Scripture that the Sacred Writers often used the word "mind" and "heart" as if they were the same.

Jesus Himself told them that "it is from men's hearts that evil intentions emerge.... Nothing that goes into a man from outside can make him unclean; it is the things that come out of a man that make him unclean. All evil things come from within and make a man unclean" (Mark 7:21, 15, 23).

One would eventually think that theft, murder, avarice, adultery, envy, and pride, originate in the mind that reasons, plans, and determines goals, but Jesus says it all comes from the heart.

When we speak of the heart, we think of love, and wherever there is love there is the possibility of hatred. It is what we love or hate that determines our course in life, and the degree in which we love or hate will determine our success or failure.

One day Jesus said to a paralytic, "Courage, my child, your sins are forgiven" (Matt. 9:2). The Scribes were incensed that Jesus forgave sins. Only God can forgive sins and their only thought was that Jesus was blaspheming. Scripture then gives us one of those instances where mind and heart are synonymous: "Knowing what was in their minds Jesus said, 'Why do you have such wicked thoughts in your hearts?'" (Matt. 9:4).

Jesus knew what they were thinking, and yet He spoke of those invisible and inaudible words as coming from the heart.

"When anyone hears the word of the Kingdom without understanding, the Evil One comes and carries off what was sown in his heart" (Matt. 13:19).

Here again Jesus speaks of the heart as a receptacle of knowledge, and yet we all realize that it is the mind, operating through the brain, that retains knowledge, reasons, and accomplishes.

Many scientists declare that a human being is legally dead when his brain stops functioning, and others maintain he is dead when his heart stops. It is a problem that will be difficult to solve both in the physical and spiritual realm. In Scripture, however, Jesus joins the two together very often and seems to indicate that as the heart pumps blood to the brain to keep it functioning in the physical realm, the three faculties of the soul, operating through the mind, are also influenced.

The heart, the symbol of love and seat of the emotions, reaches out as a light shining in the world, indicating the power of our will and the direction we have chosen to take.

No matter how often we remember His Words, or how deeply we believe in them, if those Words do not affect our heart and move that heart to love and give all to Jesus, it is nothing. St. Paul realized this when he said to the Corinthians that if he had all knowledge, gave everything he possessed to the poor, gave his body to be burned, and had the faith that moved mountains, without love, it would be as nothing (1 Cor. 13:1-3).

Paul was not speaking of an emotional love—a love that was fanned into a raging blaze and then quickly turned into ashes. No, he was speaking of a deep love of the heart, an inner conviction, a total consecration, a drive that preferred death to denial.

The heart of the Christian was a heart of flesh, penetrated by the Spirit of the Lord. It was a heart ever aware of being a "home" in which the Spirit of the Lord reigned and loved.

The disciples going to Emmaus had this experience when Jesus began to walk beside them. After they recognized Him in the breaking of bread, they said to each other, "Did not our hearts burn within us as He talked to us on the road and explained the Scriptures to us?" (Luke 24:32).

Loving Jesus was a heart experience just as much as an intellectual acceptance of Him as Lord and Savior. This is what gave these converts life and joy. They became Lovers of God and faithful children, besides obedient subjects.

They loved Him and He loved them. They dwelt in Him as He dwelt in them through the power of the Holy Spirit.

Jesus had assured them that "a good man draws what is good from the store of goodness in his heart.... For a man's words flow out of what fills his heart" (Luke 6:45). They were to be vigilant and not permit anything to enter the door of their souls that would destroy or mar its beauty. "Watch yourselves," He told them, "or your hearts will be coarsened with debauchery and drunkenness and the cares of life" (Luke 21:34).

Jesus puts the "cares of life" in the same category as debauchery and drunkenness. All three weaknesses occupy the mind and heart. The mind becomes possessed by them, the heart revels in them, and Jesus and the Kingdom are pushed aside as something not relevant for the moment.

The first Christians never forgot the statement Jesus made one day when He said, "Store up treasures for yourself in Heaven, where neither moth nor woodworms destroy them, and thieves cannot break in and steal. For where your treasure is, there will your heart be also" (Matt. 6:20-21).

It was of primary importance then, that they analyzed their priorities to be sure the one thing necessary—the Kingdom—was first and foremost. The first Christians' goal was to pattern their lives after the life of Jesus. They were sons of God through grace, and they made sure that sin would not take that treasure away from them. However, their lives as Christians were more positive than negative. They not only safeguarded their treasure; they *increased* it every day by seizing every opportunity to grow into the likeness of Jesus. Their whole life was spent setting their hearts aright and changing those hearts to resemble Jesus.

"Shoulder My yoke, and learn from Me, for I am gentle and humble in heart, and you will find rest for your souls" (Matt. 11:29-30). The Father had given each of them the yoke of obeying the Commandments, and especially the new one—to love their neighbor as He loved them. Jesus took that yoke upon Himself when He became man, and He bore it by being meek and humble of heart.

The first Christians were to learn how to preserve their hearts' treasure by doing as Jesus did always and everywhere. The realization of the existence of Heaven detached them from the world. The words of Jesus gave them something to hang on to when the going was difficult, but they needed a heart united to the very heart of God to persevere in maintaining and increasing their treasure in Heaven.

The Heart of Jesus gave the souls of these Christians peace and rest. The Apostles often related to them how, when Jesus appeared to them after the Resurrection, He said, "Peace be with you! Why are you so agitated, and why are these doubts rising in your hearts?" (Luke 24:39).

Like the Apostles before them, the first Christians had to fight doubt and fear many times, but they would unite their hearts to His. They would love as He loved and have the same goal and determination as He.

He came as Light, and they would be the radiation of that Light. He showed mankind the Father's Love, and they would be an example of that Love. He was detached and never lost sight of His Father, and they would be detached and never lose sight of Him. As Jesus manifested the Father, they would manifest Jesus.

Jesus said He only did what He saw the Father do. The first Christians strove with all their power to do as Jesus did. "The proof," Paul told them, "that you are sons is that God has sent the Spirit of His Son into our hearts — the Spirit that cries, 'Abba, Father'" (Gal. 4:6).

They were to be patient and persevere in being like Jesus. They were to be, "happy, always happy in the Lord, full of peace, guarding their hearts and thoughts in Christ Jesus" (Phil. 4:4, 7). Their hearts were to belong to Jesus; He was their first love; He was the center of their day, their life, their work, their goal. He was truly the heart of their hearts, and they safeguarded this treasure with determination and zeal.

They kept His words in their minds and His Love in their hearts, and together they changed their lives, "so that Christ might live in their hearts through faith, and then, planted in love and built in love, they would begin to understand the Infinite Love of God, as He gave them His very Spirit to dwell in their hearts" (Eph. 3:16-20).

Their lives were living witnesses of the love of Jesus. St. Paul told them, "You are a letter from Christ, drawn up by us and written, not with ink, but with the Spirit of the living Christ; not on stone tablets, but on the tablets of your living hearts" (2 Cor. 3:3).

Prayer of Anguish

The first Christians experienced moments of ecstasy, hours of happiness, a perpetual joy, and deep anguish of heart. Life for them changed, but the change for the better was within. Although their inner self was more important, their life in the world clamored for attention and often caused them their greatest pain.

It is always painful to change anything, and perhaps the greatest pain of all is the loneliness of change. This was the first deep pain the Christians experienced. They suddenly stood alone in the world as strangers. Everything and everyone was different and many times opposed to their way of thinking and living.

Only a short time ago they were comfortable in the world, but when Jesus entered their hearts they were cut off from that world and became as foreigners in a land of exile.

Many times they had to recall the words of Jesus, "If the world hates you, remember that it hated Me before you.... My choice withdrew you from the world.... I am not asking You, Father, to remove them from the world, but to protect them from the Evil One" (John 15:18-19; 17:15). The Christians had something glorious within them, something they talked about, shared, and struggled for, but they could not give it to anyone. It was a gift, and that gift of Faith spread by its manifestation in their lives.

It was a great trial for them to realize that the very love in their hearts created a separation from former friends and divided father from son and daughter from mother. They looked to Jesus and realized that His life, too, was a sign of contradiction. His very Presence in a crowd divided it immediately into two groups, those who loved Him and those who hated Him.

Like Jesus, they prayed for their persecutors, but their prayers were mixed with tears and sorrow. While their lips moved in pleas for mercy, their hearts burned within them with love for Jesus. They realized with Paul that nothing could come between them and Christ, even if they were worried or troubled or persecuted or lacking food and clothing. They were threatened and attacked, but God would turn everything to their good because they loved Him (Rom. 8:31-39).

When Jesus told Ananias He would show Paul how much he would suffer for His Name, Paul had no idea what Jesus meant. Years later he realized only too well that his greatest trial was alienation from those he loved. "It seems to me," Paul told the Corinthians, "God has put us Apostles at the end of His Parade.... We have been put on show in front of the whole universe.... We are nobodies.... We go without food and drink and clothes; we are beaten and have no homes.... We are cursed and we answer with a blessing; when we are hounded we put up with it; we are insulted and we answer politely. We are treated as the offal of the world — the scum of the earth" (1 Cor. 4:9-13).

Paul was hated by his brethren, the Jews; he was under suspicion from the Gentiles, and he had for a time a disgusting disease that revolted all who saw him (Gal. 4:14). All the Christians were hounded as criminals and sought for as traitors, but the anguish in their hearts, severe and crushing, became a prayer.

They were suffering for the sake of His Name, and they cried out to Him and depended upon Him alone for strength and courage. Fear often gripped their souls to the point where they pleaded for deliverance but they kept their eyes on Jesus.

Jesus had warned them this life of exile would not be easy, and so they saw everything as an opportunity to raise their souls to God in heartfelt prayer. All of life was a journey.

Prayer was to raise the mind and heart to God, and as those anguished days passed on into weeks and then into years, they became stronger and more serene. Their trust was in Jesus, and they had no preconceived ideas as to how He would plan and dispose of their lives.

These Christians never separated God from everyday life. He was the cause of their anguish; He was their consolation in pain; He was the love of their lives, and they would offer to Him their distress, as well as their joy, as a pleasing sacrifice.

When their souls were fearful, they united that fear with His in the Garden of Agony. When their persecutors made them leave home and land, they merely saw the opportunity to spread the Good News in far-off places.

They listened for and to the Voice of the Spirit as He guided their lives to a fruitful conclusion.

There were many uncertainties in life, but they were all turned into a prayer. Everything remained outside of them, and the heartaches that resulted from the malice of other men made them more detached and dependent upon their Lord and Teacher.

They realized that the road between finding Jesus and arriving Home was long and arduous but His Spirit prayed in them when they did not know what to say; He guided them when they did not know the direction to take, and He loved in them when their hearts were cold and distraught. Everything was part of an eternal plan that they lived out moment to moment and used to the best advantage.

They gave themselves entirely to the Holy Spirit, and Paul voiced the sentiments of all the Christians when he said, "And now you see me a prisoner already in spirit. I am on my way to Jerusalem, but have no idea what will happen to me there, except that the Holy Spirit, in town after town, has made it

clear enough that imprisonment and persecution await me"
(Acts 20:22-23).

Paul had given himself to God in such a complete way that
he was like a prisoner to His Spirit, ever obedient to His Will,
ever ready to suffer or die for the sake of Jesus. Paul could see
more and more hatred for himself and his cause in town after
town, and he realized his time to preach the Good News was
short.

The uncertainties that brought anguish to the hearts of
these Christians also brought with them Hope and Joy. They
had a cause, a goal, a Hero, and anguish of mind was part of
the price to pay. They did not become bitter with their lot, for
they knew they would possess their souls in patience.

These Christians suffered not only from the alienation of
friends, persecution, and loss of home and land, but some of
them also had bodily illness, and desolation. There is nothing
more difficult than pain within oneself, whether that pain be
physical, spiritual, or mental. Man can withstand great trials
as long as those trials originate outside himself.

No matter how strong the battle we fight may be, as long
as our health and our hope are preserved intact, we can withstand the onslaughts. In the Old Testament, Job withstood

all the calamities that Satan visited upon him with patience, fortitude, and resignation, but when his body and soul were racked in pain, he cursed the day he was born (Job 3:1).

The first Christians were soldiers in the army of Christ and no exception to the ills of the rest of society. The Master had filled their souls with sanctifying grace, made them heirs to the Kingdom, and placed the seal of His Spirit on their foreheads at Baptism, but He did not exempt them from the consequences of original sin.

Their lives on earth remained full of toil and sweat, but were changed by the power of His Spirit through joyful acceptance of their lot, a hope for something better to come, and a sense of purpose that no suffering could dissuade.

The decadent society in which they lived made sickness and disease rampant. The Lord Jesus had given power to His Apostles to cure these illnesses, and they did, but the greatest part of the Apostles' day was spent in preaching the Word and in Prayer.

When a dispute arose concerning the distribution of food, the Apostles chose seven men, whom they called "deacons," to fulfill this ministry. They did this so they could "devote themselves to Prayer and to the service of the Word" (Acts 6:4).

So many miracles and cures were wrought by the Apostles that the "sick were taken out into the streets and laid on beds and sleeping mats, in the hope that at least the shadow of Peter might fall across some of them as he went past" (Acts 5:15).

It is strange, then, that such a man should talk to his converts about the benefits of illness. He told the Christians that, "anyone who in this life has bodily suffering, has broken with sin, because for the rest of his life on earth he is not ruled by human passions, but only by the Will of God" (1 Pet. 4:1-2).

He went on to explain that in the past many of them gave way to their passions, drinking in wild parties, and behaving indecently. It is certainly logical to see that one who is physically ill is hampered from indulging in his weaknesses. This does not indicate that all those who are physically ill are so as a precaution against sin, but it does manifest one of the many pruning benefits of illness when God permits it in our lives.

Our dear Lord Himself made a strange statement one day when His Apostles asked Him about the cause of a man being born blind. "Rabbi, who sinned, this man or his parents, for him to have been born blind?" It is certainly obvious that the man himself could not sin before he was born and Jesus told them that neither did his parents sin. "He was born blind,"

Jesus told them, "so that the works of God might be displayed in him" (John 9:1-3).

To think that the Father deliberately created this man without the faculty to see just so Jesus could cure him is to ascribe to God a monstrous act. There were and always will be defects and physical illnesses in the world, caused by natural discrepancies that would provide enough "signs" to increase the faith of His people when Jesus healed them.

The Father did not and would not create anyone deliberately defective to give His Son this opportunity to heal. The consequences of original sin and the weaknesses of the human body provided more than enough people to be cured. What then did Jesus mean?

The blind man himself had not asked Jesus to heal him. He probably had not even heard of Jesus. It was only after the man was cured and interrogated by the Pharisees that he came to believe that Jesus was the Son of God. This man had no faith in Jesus as Lord before his cure. Scripture gives us no evidence that he even desired to be healed.

Through some genetic deficiency this man was born without eyeballs and he accepted his lot humbly and patiently. This acceptance is a "work" of God, for only God can give us the grace to accept the cross with patience. Our human nature rebels against the cross, especially when that cross is physical or it means we are deprived of some faculty that is so necessary for everyday living.

It was this humble, joyful acceptance of pain, suffering, trials, and persecution that made the pagans look in awe at these followers of Jesus.

Jesus gave us two important lessons in this narrative. Firstly, it is a "work" of God to accept any cross in life with patience and love, whether that cross be imposed on us by nature, as in physical handicaps, or persecution resulting from the malice of men. Secondly, He manifested His Divinity. The Book of Genesis tells us that God made man from the slime of the earth. Jesus "spat on the ground, made a paste with the spittle, put this over the eyes of the blind man, and told him to go and wash in the Pool of Siloam." Jesus used the same material to create eyes for the man as the Father used to create Adam. The eyelids had never opened because there were no eyeballs (John 9:1-12).

This miracle was so astounding that the former blind man was brought before the Pharisees to be questioned. He was the only blind person cured by Jesus who was interrogated by those in authority. Even his parents were questioned, but all they knew was that their son was born blind, his eyes closed, and now he had eyes that could see.

For his insistence that Jesus gave him eyes to see on the Sabbath, the man was excommunicated from the synagogue. Jesus heard of it and went to look for him. It was only when Jesus asked if he believed in the "Son of Man" that he did believe and knelt down to worship Him.

These first Christians were not exempt from the illnesses and physical pain that is so much a part of this world. They realized that, like the blind man, there was a time for healing and a time for pain, and both gave glory to God. Both increased their glory in the Kingdom.

There were times when they were forced to leave everything and flee to other towns to escape death and persecution. It was especially at times like these that they suffered from hunger, thirst, exposure to the elements, and contaminated water. Though God protected them from many misfortunes, they were not immune to every ill. They were sons of God, and like their Leader, Jesus, they were to show the world how to live without discouragement and despair amidst these evils.

They were to use common, practical means to preserve their health, pray for the continuation of that health, and then go their way in peace, knowing that their Father knew what was for their good. They trusted Him. It was Timothy who showed us how these Christians were to look at illness, for St. Paul gave him some practical advice in his needs.

Realizing that drinking water was often contaminated with sewage, Paul told him, "You should give up drinking only water, and have a little wine for the sake of your digestion and the frequent bouts of illness that you have" (1 Tim. 5:23).

Timothy was obviously acquainted with physical suffering, and the man who healed many and raised a young boy from the dead, merely gave him some homey advice to bear it all patiently.

Paul himself mentions his own weaknesses and a disgusting disease, neither of which were taken from him as far as the Scriptures report. When he did implore the Lord to deliver him from "weaknesses, insults, hardships, persecutions, and the agonies" he went through for the sake of Jesus, the Lord replied that His "power was at its best in weakness" (2 Cor. 12:7-10).

This was one of the most important lessons the first Christians learned. Weakness, illness, frustration, tension, and anxiety were no longer enemies to their souls; they were now used to show forth the power of God in their lives. Jesus would not deliver them from trials; He would give them inner power to overcome those trials, be joyful in the midst of them, and turn them into merit for the Kingdom to come. These frustrations would be turned into precious jewels in Heaven.

They had the power of His Spirit within them, and they never had to fear the vicissitudes of life.

When they hid in the catacombs in order to Break Bread and worship, they did so with a sense of finality. Every night new converts joined their ranks as others were taken prisoner or martyred.

Some of them left for other places and preached the Good News everywhere. The more they were persecuted, the greater number of people joined their ranks and the more love poured out from them. Their way of life and their love was fed by sacrifice and persecution.

They were children of God and slaves to no one. They were free, and though anxiety became part of their daily lives, it was no longer a burden but a test of their courage, confidence, and trust in Jesus. They learned how to cope with every situation and turn darkness into light, and anxiety into serenity.

Paul gave them courage and light when he told them, "I know how to be poor and I know how to be rich. I have been through my initiation and now I am ready for anything anywhere—full stomach or empty stomach, poverty or plenty. There is nothing I cannot master with the help of the One who gives me strength" (Phil. 4:11-12).

Yes, trials, illness, and persecution were their initiation, and they strove to pass the test with love, joy, peace, and trust. To the world, anxiety was frustration; to the first Christians, it was exaltation.

St. Paul's life seemed to be wrapped in anguish. He began his career as a persecutor determined and ill at ease until every last Christian was in jail or slain. His conversion resulted in days of distress as he realized that his zeal was misplaced and Jesus was truly God and Lord.

For seventeen years he prayed and studied his new faith and then found himself still feared and under suspicion. Everywhere he traveled, he had to fear his life. His enemies among his own were numerous, and they often followed him to discredit everything he said.

His Apostleship was constantly questioned by fellow Christians and he had to defend his right to that title by telling them that he was a true Apostle for he had seen the Lord and exhibited the power of His Spirit by mighty deeds.

Not only by his deeds did he have to prove he was an Apostle but by his suffering for the faith. He had to work harder, was in prison, flogged, beaten, and shipwrecked more often than anyone else (2 Cor. 11:22-29).

He was in constant danger everywhere and from everything, including "rivers and the open sea." Most of all his "anxiety for all the churches" and his fear of error in their ranks forced him to warn the Christians over and over again. "Be on your guard," he told them. "I know quite well that when I have gone, fierce wolves will invade you and will have no mercy on the flock" (Acts 20:28-29).

Peter, too, had his moments of anguish. His terrible fall ever made him wary of his own strength and forced him to depend entirely on the Lord Jesus.

This man of repentance and compassion for his neighbors was forced one day to make an example of two people who tried to deceive the newly formed Christian community. Ananias and Sapphira were struck dead for lying to the Holy Spirit when Peter questioned the sale of their property (Acts 5:1-11).

He had to reprove Simon for trying to buy power. "May your silver be lost forever, and you with it, for thinking that money could buy what God has given for nothing" (Acts 8:20). Though Peter spoke under the influence of the Spirit these occasions were full of tension and anguish of heart. To see men selfish in the things of God causes untold distress in the hearts of those who have given their entire selves to His service.

The wrath of the Pharisees and the numerous Christians martyred by pagan emperors, gave Peter great concern and compassion for all those who suffered for Jesus' Name.

And then one day Peter had a vision that was to cause him many an anguished hour. He saw heaven open and a large sheet lowered that contained every possible sort of animal. He was told to eat and soon realized that God was about to change his lifestyle.

Peter was told by this symbolic vision that the Apostles were to preach to and baptize the Gentiles, for Jesus came to save all men. The first convert was an Italian centurion named Cornelius and although to us it seems of little consequence it was not so for a pious Jew.

Peter always felt criticism keenly, and after the conversion of Cornelius he received a deluge of reproofs from the

Apostles and the brethren in Judea. He had to explain his vision and the power of the Spirit manifested in these pagans to pacify them.

Peter and the other Apostles were faithful Israelites and entrenched in the Law. They loved Jesus and believed in His Word, but Jesus had not told them what to do about pagans. Did not Jesus Himself tell a Canaanite woman that He had been sent to the House of Israel and it wasn't right to give the bread of children to dogs? (Matt. 15:25-26).

The brethren's acceptance of His vision was temporary, and Peter became more and more in doubt as to his course. This uncertainty caused him many anguished hours. He prayed and continued to associate with pagans and baptize them. And then one day the inevitable clash came — the clash in which God's Will became clear and Peter's prayer for light was answered.

To solve his dilemma, Peter began to compromise. James and his friends began to teach that pagans must first be Jews before they became Christians. They put pressure on Peter, and he succumbed. "His custom had been to eat with the pagans, but after certain friends of James arrived, he stopped doing this and kept away from them altogether, for fear of the group that insisted on circumcision" (Gal. 2:11-12).

Paul and Barnabas had a long argument with them. At this time Paul said, "When I saw they were not respecting the true meaning of the Good News, I said to Cephas in front of everyone, 'In spite of being a Jew, you live like the pagans and not like the Jews, so you have no right to make pagans copy Jewish ways'" (Gal. 2:14).

It is interesting at this point to observe the action of real Christians in a heated discussion. They all decided to go to Jerusalem and present the problem to a Council of Apostles and elders. It was in such an assembly that the Spirit would speak.

These men were dealing with a problem that caused each conflicting side anguish of heart. Each felt he was doing God's Will and adhered to his opinion. The difference between them and ourselves is that they sought guidance, prayed, and were objective in their opinions.

Though each side was strong in their opinions, they listened and had the humility of heart to change when God's Will was manifested.

Men of prayer may have doubts, but they never lose faith or confidence in the guiding hand of God in their lives. Though they were men of great discernment, the solutions to their problems did not always come quickly like a flash of light. They traveled ordinary ways and had to wait with patience and perseverance for God to show them the way.

Peter's vacillating temperament had manifested itself again, but unlike the incident in the Courtyard when he denied his Master, this time he listened, waited, and prayed. His weakness was still there but he learned how to cope with it. His heart had told him that Gentiles were not to become Jews, but his mind had given in to fear. He made no final decision until he knew the Will of God.

After a long discussion, Peter stood up and told the community gathered in Jerusalem that they had no right to impose the Old Law on the pagans. God is no respecter of persons. He sent His Spirit to pagans as well as Jews. Peter's discourse was eloquent and so filled with the Holy Spirit that all were silent.

It was at this point that the real Christian status of these men was apparent. James, the man most opposed to Peter's and Paul's arguments, rose up and told all those present that it was not just making a pagan follow Mosaic Laws before he became a Christian.

The Spirit brought to the mind of James a passage from the Prophet Amos where the Lord God said that pagans would be consecrated to His Name (Acts 15:16-18).

James then ruled that a letter be sent to the new Christians asking them merely to observe some dietary rules to keep them from pagan sacrifices.

The letter written to these early Christians was short, but it portrayed a quality of soul and faith unknown today. Strong-minded men had deep differences of opinion on an explosive subject, but they prayed to God and listened to His Spirit in one another. They all suffered from the rift that occurred when their disagreements became more and more apparent. Their sincerity and determination to find God's Will made them say to the Christians, "It has been decided by the Holy Spirit and by ourselves not to saddle you with any burden beyond these essentials" (Acts 15:28).

Anguish of heart did not make these men lose sight of the Holy Spirit. They found Him in the midst of tribulations and distress, and like Paul they could say, "I am quite content with my weaknesses, insults, hardships, persecution, and the agonies I go through for Christ's sake, for it is when I am weak that I am strong" (2 Cor. 12:10).

Prayer of Humility

The pagans that Paul converted were, for the most part, immoral renegades, the scum of humanity. They had reached a level of depravity known only to those who have been there. They had no concept of life after death or a loving God. Life was an endurance test and a challenge to see how much pleasure could be squeezed out of every miserable moment.

This was the atmosphere at Corinth when Paul went there to preach the Good News. He performed so many miracles and wonders that people would vie with one another for a handkerchief or piece of his apron so the sick could be touched with his clothing and healed (Acts 19:11-12). Paul told them about Jesus, and they saw in Paul a power and a strength they had never seen before.

When they realized that God loved them enough to send His own Son to redeem them and His Spirit to make them heirs, they left their old ways and began to live saintly lives.

They experienced great joy and peace — a peace they never dreamed possible. They were completely caught up in this new experience and this new way of life.

Peter, a man of experience, tried to warn them. "Be calm," he said, "and vigilant, because your enemy, the devil, is prowling round like a roaring lion, looking for someone to eat" (1 Pet. 5:8). But many of them began to relax their vigilance, and slowly, imperceptibly, they began to slide back to their former ways.

They were attacked on every side. Some began to doubt Paul's authenticity as an Apostle; others slid back to immoral lives. False doctrines began to spread, and the argument about the law of Moses almost rent the Christian community in two.

They were looked upon as "nobodies" in the world, and the constant fear of death made some of the Christians waver in their newfound faith.

"If any one of you shall suffer for being a Christian," Peter told them, "then he is not to be ashamed of it; he should thank God that he has been called one" (1 Pet. 4:16).

Peter and Paul both had learned the Prayer of Humility well. They became wanderers going from place to place, admired by a few and despised by the crowds.

Neither of these men ever forgot their past weaknesses. Peter, the denier, and Paul, the persecutor, were well grounded in the truth that they could do nothing in themselves but all things in Him.

Because both were acquainted with failure and could correct with gentleness, they were veritable pillars of strength to the newborn Christians. The Christians who were immersed in the consolations of their faith, had the tendency to become proud of themselves and their strength.

Though they were forgiven much, and enjoyed the peace of the truly repentant, they often found forgiving their neighbor a difficult task, and had to be warned by the Apostles of their erring ways. "Wrap yourselves in humility to be servants of each other, because God refuses the proud and will always favor the humble" (1 Pet. 5:5).

When their first enthusiasm began to wear a little thin and the Lord called them to greater heights of prayer by the desert of dryness, and uncertainty, they began to look at their old ways. They wondered if they could not revert to old practices and sins and still remain Christians. Was not the total dedication to the faith a little unreal in their society? Thoughts like these ran through their minds. Some wavered, and some fell deeply into sin.

False apostles and false prophets taught their own doctrines and those Christians whose faith was built on an emotional level were swayed to new gospels. "Any newcomer has only to proclaim a new Jesus, different from the one we preached, or a new spirit, or a new gospel from the one you have already accepted, and you welcome it with open arms.... Those men are counterfeit apostles; they are dishonest workmen, disguised as apostles of Christ" (2 Cor. 11:4, 13).

These were Christians who fell not only into doctrinal errors but also yielded to immorality, laziness, and pride. Paul had strong words to say about Christians who did not live their faith. "You should not associate with a brother Christian who is leading an immoral life, or is a usurer, or idolatrous, or a slanderer, or a drunkard, or is dishonest; you should not even eat a meal with people like that" (1 Cor. 5:11).

Paul explained that he was speaking of fellow Christians, not pagans. Unbelievers did not have the example of Jesus to pattern their lives after. They did not have the Spirit dwelling within them. The pagan's sins might be hideous but not as monstrous as a Christian's who had the light but preferred the darkness.

St. Paul was a man of strong convictions, but his own sufferings made him realistic and compassionate. "If one of you misbehaves," he said, "the more spiritual of you, who set him right, should do so in a spirit of gentleness, not forgetting that you may be tempted yourselves" (Gal. 6:1).

Not everyone was to correct an erring brother—only the most spiritual, those who understood the spiritual life and the weaknesses of human nature. They were to do so in a spirit of humility, realizing they could also fall if it were not for the grace of God.

The temptations of the Enemy and the spirit of the world that surrounded them sorely tried their poor souls. The only weapon they had was Prayer—shared Prayer and private Prayer—and when they fell in spite of all their efforts they would not despair. They would use their weaknesses as tools to arrive at a deep sense of their unworthiness and the grandeur of God's Perfections.

They did fall at times, and they exhibited many imperfections, but these failures never discouraged them or made them despondent. They realized that God loved them not because they were good but because He was good and they needed Him desperately.

St. John made them realize this truth when he said, "God's love for us was revealed when God sent into the world His only Son.... This is the love I mean ... not our love for God, but God's love for us when He sent His Son to be a sacrifice that takes our sins away" (1 John 4:9-10).

How different was this concept from that of the Pharisees. These men thought they had to be good first and then they deserved God's love in return. "I thank You, God, that I am not like the rest of men" said one of them in the Temple (Luke 18:11).

He did not realize in his pride that it was precisely in *being* like the rest of men that He was loved by God. It was God who took the initiative and had pity on sinners — sinners who struck their breasts and said, "Oh, God, be merciful to me" (Luke 18:13).

"We are to love, then, because He loved us first" (1 John 4:19). How true this was in the lives of the Apostles and the first Christians. The Prophets of old like Isaias and Jeremias were sanctified in their mother's womb, as was John the Baptist. Elias and Eliseus lived frugal and penitential lives in the desert in an effort to maintain a personal contact with God.

When Jesus came, however, He began by picking out imperfect "uneducated laymen" (Acts 4:13) who constantly bickered about their place at table and in the Kingdom — men ambitious for honor and glory with little comprehension of a spiritual life.

One Apostle was a despised tax collector, and many were Galileans, whose speech betrayed their ignorance. The only respected "Judean" was Judas, who turned traitor.

It was as if God were trying to prove from the very beginning that He chose us; we did not choose Him (John 15:16). Even after Pentecost God continued this pattern by giving Saul the charism of seeing His Light, hearing His voice, and being knocked from his horse — all while he was a sinner and persecutor.

God looked down upon poor sinners and placed into their hearts His own Spirit so they might look upon Him as sons look upon their father. It was nothing they merited, nothing they deserved. It was all His Goodness reaching down from His mighty Throne and lifting up their nature to a state beyond their wildest dreams.

"We were still helpless when at His appointed moment Christ died for sinful men.... What proves that God loves us is that Christ died for us while we were still sinners" (Rom. 5:6, 8). Paul wanted to impress upon his converts the depths and goodness of God's love for them. They had to realize that God loved them when they were in a state of rebellion against Him.

Now that they were converted, changed, and made new by the Spirit of God, they had to manifest their sonship by bearing the fruit of humility. This humility was not a downgrading of their identity. It was a deep awareness of the depths of God's all-embracing, personal love for each one of them with all their weaknesses and frailties.

They were, in the mind of the world, most unlikely subjects for the love of an Omnipotent God, and that was the beauty of it all. They were unlovable creatures on whom God's loving eyes looked with Mercy and Compassion.

When they were chosen by that Love they were neither wise, influential, nor noble. It was to shame the wise that God chose what was foolish in the eyes of the world. They were common and contemptible as the world judges its children. This was their boast. To shame the strong, God chose the weak. To show up those who had everything, He chose those who had nothing. He did all this because He Himself would be their wisdom and virtue and holiness and freedom (1 Cor. 1:26-31).

He would live in them, and the remembrance of their little-
ness would make His power more manifest, His love more gratuitous, and His grace more precious.

To the pagans, these Christians were a contradiction. It
would be human and natural to despair at the sight of one's
frailties, but they saw the opposite effect in Christians who
rejoiced at their weaknesses.

It would be human to want to do everything oneself, but
the Christians found joy in the realization that they had no
power and that the power of Jesus bore more fruit in them.

They were once slaves to sin and at times they had to en-
gage in a fierce battle to retain their newfound freedom, but,
come what may, they would use every precious moment of
time and every situation as a stepping-stone to the Kingdom.

They followed the Lord with the same determination with
which they had once followed a life of sin. "As once you put
your bodies at the service of vice and immorality," St. Paul
reminded them, "so now you must put them at the service of
righteousness for your sanctification" (Rom. 6:19).

There was in their nature a constant struggle for the freedom of a child of God. They were ever conscious of something
in the depths of their souls that sought sin while another force,

even deeper, cried out for goodness, virtue, and truth. It was a lonely battle waged between invisible forces that sometimes won and sometimes lost.

Their hearts reached out for holiness, and their minds loved the Commandments of their Lord, but in spite of all this there was always that intangible, invisible something that made them do what they did not want to do. It was a habit of sin they had formed and that came to them so quickly they often stood back in awe at their weaknesses.

"Though the will to do what is good is in me," St. Paul told them, "the performance is not, with the result that instead of doing the good things I want to do, I carry out the sinful things I do not want. When I act against my will, then, it is not my true self doing it, but sin which lives in me" (Rom. 7:18-20).

Paul had to admit that this behavior seemed to be the rule in his life. "Every single time I want to do good, it is something evil that comes to hand" (Rom. 7:21), he told his converts. But with one thought and one stroke of his pen, Paul told the first Christians how to solve this dilemma and contradiction. "What a wretched man I am! Who will rescue me from this body doomed to death? Thanks be to God through Jesus Christ, our Lord!" (Rom. 7:24-25).

He tells them that our reasoning power and our will power are weak, but thanks to God, Jesus came into a body like ours in order to condemn sin. Now, he explained, they were to live by the Spirit, and not by the body. Since the Spirit of God had made His home in them, they were to behave as He dictated and inspired (Rom. 8:1-11).

They were to remember that they were dead to sin and were to live a life according to the Spirit, and it was only because of this Spirit that they would be free and at peace. Unless the Spirit of Jesus possessed their souls, they would not belong to God because "everyone moved by the Spirit is a son to God, and this Spirit in them made them cry out 'Abba, Father'" (Rom. 8:14-15).

The struggle within them became a prayer — the Prayer of Humility. They were to decrease, and He was to increase. They were to live spiritual lives in the Spirit and give up the habit of sin in their bodies.

In their very weaknesses the Spirit would come and help them for when they were weary in the struggle He would express their pleas in a way that could never be put into words and God, who knew their hearts and their desires would know what they needed (Rom. 8:26-27).

The fight to let the Spirit rule was at times painful, disappointing, and heartrending. There were battles they won and battles they lost, but slowly and imperceptibly they changed and bore fruit a hundredfold. The struggle for holiness bore the fruit of Jesus, for like Him, they were meek and humble of heart, ruled by His Spirit, called "sons of God," and visible images of their Lord on earth. His Power was truly at its best in their weakness.

The Prayer of Hope

Humility is a liberating virtue, for it takes away from the soul the burden of any injustice. It gives us the freedom to leave everything in God's hands and the contentment to be satisfied with His plan in our lives.

Humility is an exhilarating virtue that keeps us from discouragement at the sight of our frailties. It is coupled with Hope in an indissoluble union, and together they bring our souls to great heights of holiness.

The first Christians were not afraid to remember their past. Humility covered it like a blanket. Neither did they fear the future, for Hope lit the way and they were assured the path would lead directly to God.

They knew that Faith, Love, and Grace were gifts from God, and Hope gave them the assurance that the invisible reality was their possession now. They had only to correspond with these gifts and give the Spirit the freedom to work in their lives.

The Father had given them the greatest gift of all—His Son—and He would not refuse them lesser gifts.

The first Christians possessed a tremendous sense of expectation for the glorious gifts reserved for them at the Second Coming and in Heaven. Their Hope gave them the enthusiasm to look forward to His coming with eagerness. Salvation meant the resurrection of the body, the fullness of the gifts of the Spirit, the inheritance of sons of God, the glory of the Kingdom and the eternal embrace of God, their Father.

They knew that in their lives they had already begun this glorious heritage by sharing the greatest gift of all—the Holy Spirit. Unlike the hope in the Old Testament, which was an expectation of something to come, the hope the first Christians possessed made their Heaven begin here and now by the fact that they were the Temples of the Spirit.

Their hope was secure because it was based on God Himself, who gave them His Son. He invited them to go to Him through Jesus. He manifested His love by giving His Son's life for their Redemption and then releasing the power of His Spirit to fill their hearts.

Their lives were full of the joy of realizing that someday their bodies would rise and Jesus would come again and show the whole world that He was Lord.

In order to appreciate the kind of Hope these Christians possessed, we will look at its various aspects and see how it kept them in a spirit of Prayer.

Expectant Hope

It is important to remember that the Hope the first Christians possessed was based on a promise fulfilled. Unlike the Hope of Abraham, who waited for something to come, they saw the promise of the Father made manifest in Jesus. The life of Jesus gave them concrete proof of what lay in store for them.

He was their Hope fulfilled, and so they did not need to be men of desires but men of expectation. Although their eyes had not seen the Glory to come, they did know the Source of that Glory—Jesus. They "felt" His Presence in their souls. They "saw" His Power manifested by great and marvelous works in His Apostles.

His own Spirit spoke to them in the depths of their souls and guided their lives with a loving Providence. They were like children looking to their Father for guidance, love, and protection, and His Presence surrounded them with an abiding sense of expectant Hope.

"Blessed be God, the Father of our Lord, Jesus Christ," Saint Peter told them, "who, in His great Mercy, has given us a new birth as His sons, by raising Jesus Christ from the dead so that we have a *sure* Hope, and the promise of an inheritance that can never be spoilt or soiled, and never fade away, because it is kept for you in the Heavens" (1 Pet. 1:3-4).

"You did not see Him," Peter told them, "yet you love Him; and still without seeing Him, you are already filled with a joy so glorious that it cannot be described, because you believe; and you are sure of the end to which your faith looks forward, that is, the salvation of your souls" (1 Pet. 1:8-9).

The word "sure" describes what the Apostle expected of the first Christians. Their Hope was not a "waiting" Hope, but a "sure" Hope. It was Faith that made them look forward, but

Hope made them sure, positive, and expectant of the possession of God in His Glory.

These Christians looked forward to the Second Coming and to Heaven with a greater enthusiasm than we do for feast days, jubilees, holidays, and Christmas. We look forward to the pleasure and joy of a feast that comes and goes, but they looked forward to that Eternal Banquet that would one day come but never go.

This Hope in them was so great that it brought upon them persecution and distress. Paul told King Agrippa, "And now it is for my Hope in the promise made by God to our ancestors that I am on trial.... For that Hope, I am actually put on trial by Jews! Why does it seem incredible to you that God should raise the dead?" (Acts 26:7-8). "It is on account of the Hope of Israel that I wear this chain" (Acts 28:20).

The Resurrection of Jesus was the foundation of their Hope, and because they were sons of God through Grace, they too would rise from the grave. This realization took away the fear of death. Their souls would enjoy the Beatific Vision, and then on the last day, their mortal bodies would rise and be reunited in a glorious state forever.

It is difficult for most of us, who have been born and raised in the concept of eternal life, to fully realize what it meant to hear and believe this truth for the first time. Their souls would never die—only pass over from one mode of existence to another; they would never cease to be. What a thrill that truth must have been for these new Christians!

"Yes," Paul told the Roman Governor, "there will be a resurrection of good men and bad men alike" (Acts 24:15). "We believe that Jesus died and rose again, and that it will be the same for those who have died in Jesus, God will bring them with Him."

These Christians were so excited over the prospect of rising from the dead as Jesus did that they began to wonder what would happen if they were alive when Jesus came again. When would He come? Would it be soon? Maybe tomorrow?

St. Paul told them at the trumpet of God, the Archangel would call out the command and Jesus would come down with all those who died in Him, and those who were living at that time would "be taken up in the clouds together with those that are risen, and meet the Lord in the air" (1 Thess. 4:16-17).

These Christians were curious about time and place. Paul, like Jesus, told them not to expect to know "times and seasons for the Day of the Lord is going to come like a thief in the night" (1 Thess. 5:1-2).

They were to live in the "light" and not like those who had no faith and hope. God had enlightened their minds to know with a certainty that He would come again, and like Him, they would rise from the grave. Faith and Love were their shield and Hope their helmet. Their souls were to be united to Jesus in such an intimate way that it would make no difference whether they lived during that glorious coming or not (1 Thess. 5:7-8).

Living with God was to be a "now" experience, and they were to be ready at any time the Master would call. This time of waiting was to be filled with good works and interior change. It was not a time for idle waiting and speculation. They were to give courage to the apprehensive, take care for the weak, and be patient with everyone. Most of all, they were to "pray constantly" by being happy in the Lord, and giving thanks for every detail in their life situation (1 Thess. 5:12, 18).

Hope — The Inheritance of the Saints

This Hope made the Christians realize that salvation was possible and "possible for the whole human race" (Titus 2:11).

This was their main "work" in life — the putting on of Jesus Christ by the imitation of His life. Hope gave them the realization that they were called to be holy just as much as Abraham, the Prophets, Peter, and Paul.

They had a calling that was just as important as Abraham's, and like those specially chosen, they had to give up everything that did not lead them to God. They were a chosen people set aside and paid for by the Blood of Jesus.

"He sacrificed Himself," Paul reminded them, "in order to set us free from all wickedness and to purify a people so that it could be His very own and would have no ambition except to do good" (Titus 2:14).

It wasn't because of any good action on their part that He chose them. No, it was the compassion of the Father, the love of Jesus, and the power of His Spirit that brought them up from a life of slavery into a life of Grace and made them brothers of the Saints, heirs that looked forward to inheriting the land of their Father.

They were God's children and they looked upon this dignity with gratitude and humility. It was real to them and although they had not seen the glory of their Home, they had Hope that gave them a glimpse into that invisible realm.

They would see God as He really was and that experience would place their souls and eventually their bodies in a state of joy that was inexpressible in human language.

Being a child and heir gave them an awareness of love they had never known before, and it was fed by Hope. That love reached out to their neighbor and made that neighbor also desire to belong to God's family.

Hope made the word "chosen" mean something very special in their lives. It made them reach further, work harder, give up more, and love much. It put joy on their faces, laughter on their lips, and a song in their hearts.

They possessed His Spirit; they were His Temple; they would live and breathe by that Spirit and "be holy just as He is holy" (1 John 3:7).

Lest their hope degenerate into presumption, Paul warned them, "We must be content to hope that we shall be saved; our salvation is not in sight; we should not have to be hoping for it if it were, but, as I say, we must hope to be saved since we are not saved yet; it is something we must wait for with patience" (Rom. 8:24-25).

This was not a contradiction to his doctrine that we are saved by our faith in Jesus. He wanted his converts to understand that without a change of life, an adherence to His word, and a deep love for their neighbor, salvation would not be theirs.

The basis of their Faith was that Jesus is Lord. He was sent by the Father, lived, died, and rose from the grave. Because He is Lord, His life, sufferings, death, and Resurrection merited for mankind the forgiveness of their sins, and made them like Him — sons of God. This had to go beyond the "knowledge" stage and affect their lives in a radical, dramatic way.

The knowledge of an historical Jesus was not enough, for the Enemy possesses the knowledge that Jesus is Lord and he is not saved. It is his very belief and rejection of that knowledge that creates his hell. He will not accept Jesus as Lord in his life. His pride recoils at the realization that the Son of God assumed our human nature and became Man — God-Man. This knowledge and his rebellion against it is pride — the kind of pride that puts itself above the Wisdom of God, and says, "I will not serve" (Jer. 2:20).

So, the mere knowledge or belief that Jesus is Lord is not sufficient for salvation. When Paul told the Christians that faith in Jesus saved them and John told them that whoever believed that Jesus is Lord is saved, they were encouraging a change of lifestyle. "Do not model yourselves on the behavior of the world around you," Paul told them, "but let your behavior change, modeled by your new mind. This is the only way to discover the Will of God and know what is good, what it is that He wants, what is the perfect thing to do.... Do not let your love be a pretense, but sincerely prefer good to evil.... Do not allow yourselves to become self-satisfied" (Rom. 12:2, 9, 16).

St. John made some startling statements in regard to his concept of what it means to believe in Jesus — the Jesus who saves. He told his converts that they were to be "pure as Christ." To live a holy life, he told them, "is to be holy as He is holy.... Anyone not living a holy life, and not loving his brother, is no child of God's.... Or love is not to be just words or mere talk, but something real and active: only by this can we be certain that we are children of the Truth" (1 John 3:3, 10, 18).

It is only through Jesus that we enter the Kingdom, for He merited grace for our souls so we may see the Face of our Father. This means we must be like Him and in the measure our faith changes us, in that measure shall we be like Him. Our belief in Jesus as Lord must affect the conduct of our lives, or we shall be accused of being children of light and preferring darkness.

This is very evident in the lives of the Apostles. They all began by believing that Jesus was the son of God — the expected One. Eleven of these men believed and changed, even though at times they fell through their weaknesses. But Judas rebelled against change in his life, and that rebellion turned love into hatred—hatred that was not satisfied until the Man he once loved was destroyed.

All twelve believed Jesus was the Messiah, but the belief of Judas stopped short at the need to change, and he destroyed his Lord. For a moment, Peter's faith stopped short, and he denied his Lord, but love triumphed and he repented. Peter remembered that Jesus foretold his denial, but he also remembered His admonition, "Once you have recovered, you in your turn must strengthen your brothers" (Luke 22:32). Peter was to use his failure to further his determination to change his own life and to help others change their lives.

This does not mean that anything we do or become has the power to save us; it only means that we must cooperate with the Holy Spirit and His grace and inspirations.

God has given and chosen but we must accept and respond. His love is gratuitous and infinite, and we must reciprocate with all the love we possess. He desires all men to be holy, to be saved, but He will not force us to be holy or to love Him. It is a union of love and wills that fills us with Him and empties us of ourselves. He must increase and we must decrease, but somehow in the process we find our true selves—that self that He created to His image and likeness, that self that sin has disfigured and weakness disabled, that self that has been reborn and made glorious by the Precious Blood of Jesus.

Yes, these first Christians were under no illusions. They knew what God had done for them and what they were to do in return, and together they formed a partnership that continued on into eternity.

Hope of Eternal Glory

There was one aspect of Hope that the first Christians learned quickly, and that was the need to persevere. Jesus had told them one time that a man who began to build a house he could not finish would be laughed at by his neighbors (Luke 14:28-29).

The more they formed the habit of being like Jesus, the holier they became; and the longer they persevered in this path, the greater became their Hope. St. Paul told them, "We can boast about looking forward to God's glory. But that is not all we can boast about; we can boast about our sufferings. These sufferings bring patience, and patience brings perseverance, and perseverance brings Hope, and this Hope is not deceptive because the love of God has been poured into our hearts by the Holy Spirit" (Rom. 5:3-5).

God Himself, through His Holy Spirit, was the source of their Hope. He it was who bore fruit in them—fruit that lasted. Jesus made this clear during the Last Supper discourse. "I commission you to go out and bear fruit," He said, "fruit that will last" (John 15:16).

Unlike the people of the world who are good one day and bad the next, the Christians, who bore within their souls the very Spirit of God, persevered in bearing fruit by the very stumbling block that made those of the world fall, that is—Suffering.

Persecutions, hardships, and sickness were not occasions of discouragement and despair—they were occasions to imitate, to bear fruit, to rise above, and to exhibit joyful detachment. These things, cheerfully borne, made them patient. The less they "kicked against the goad" (Acts 26:14), the more control they possessed of every situation.

They became less and less frantic at every disappointment because, like Jesus, they saw the Father's Providence in everything. Life had a purpose and a goal and a challenge hidden within its very existence. They were not going to be like those who "beat the air." They would make every moment count for eternity and add to the glory of that Heavenly place.

Selfishness was not the motive of their anticipating the glory to come. It was the joy of children, grateful to their Father for His beneficent Providence, that made them look forward to what was to come. God Himself would help them to use everything to that very end. St. Paul encouraged them in this way by saying that, "We know that by turning everything to their good, God cooperates with all those who love Him, with all those that He has called according to His purpose"—chose to become true images of His Son—"those He called He justified, and with those He justified, He shared His Glory" (Rom. 8:28-30).

They would share in the very Glory of God because Jesus came down and paved a way for them, marked it with His Precious Blood, and walked its path so they would follow in His footsteps.

Yes, Paul realized that "Hope would make them rejoice" because it was rooted in the One who would one day share His Glory with them. On earth they were "envoys of God," "letters of Christ to the world"—confident because the Spirit living within them would give their souls a "brightness and a splendor" beyond their wildest dreams (Rom. 12:12; 2 Cor. 3:3, 9).

When Moses went up the mountain to speak to God, his face shone with such splendor that the Israelites could not look upon him. What man ever read that account and did not desire that kind of holiness—so bright, so glorious, that it shone like the sun?

Paul, however, tells his Christians that because of Jesus and the grace of the Spirit in them, the Splendor of Moses is as nothing! "Compared with this greater Splendor, the thing that used to have such splendor, now seems to have none" (2 Cor. 3:10).

When Paul describes the splendor of the soul of a Christian, one feels he is in the Presence of God. He compares the brightness of Moses as something outside of him, a glory that spoke to the people like a charism. It manifested in a dramatic way that Moses had truly spoken to God.

The splendor of the Christian soul however, was greater, for that very God dwelt in his soul and changed him into Jesus. This splendor worked wonders and continually they grew brighter. Paul could only describe it by saying, "We, with our unveiled faces, reflecting like mirrors the brightness of the

Lord, all grow brighter and brighter as we are turned into the Image that we reflect; this is the work of the Lord who is Spirit" (2 Cor. 3:18).

They were not only *in* His Presence as Moses but that Presence was *within* them and Its Power transformed them into Jesus—into sons of God—living mirrors of God. They had a sublime mission, "to radiate the light of the knowledge of God's Glory, the Glory on the face of Christ" (2 Cor. 4:6).

Because "earthenware jars" held this treasure, they realized that this power to transform them came from God. They knew that many times they would find themselves in "difficulties on every side but never cornered; they could see no answer to their problems but they never despaired; and they were persecuted but never deserted" (2 Cor. 4:7-9).

The "inner man was renewed day by day," and there was a purpose in it all. "Yes," Paul told them, "the troubles which are soon over, though they weigh little, train us for the carrying of a weight of eternal glory which is out of all proportion to them" (2 Cor. 4:16-17).

As Christians, they were to live in Heaven all the way to Heaven. Because they had died to the things of this world, they were to "look for the things that are in Heaven, where

Christ is, sitting at God's right hand." "Their thoughts were to be on heavenly things and not the things of earth" because "when Christ is revealed, they, too, would be revealed in all their glory with Him" (Col. 3:1-4).

They were truly destined to share His glory, and no one would ever take away that Hope, for it came from God and led them to God.

Prayer of Thanksgiving and Praise

It is from a hopeful heart that thanksgiving flows. The first Christians were ever grateful for every gift they received, and their gratitude was enhanced by the fact that they were the recipients of a participation in the very Nature of God, without any merit on their part.

Unlike the proud of the world, who feel they deserve every good thing, these Christians sought God like a wounded deer runs for water, and when that "living water" came and healed them, their hearts sang a never-ending song of thanksgiving.

Their lips uttered soft whispers of "Thank You, God" every time His healing Spirit covered their souls with Mercy and forgiveness. Their hearts beat out a rhythmic tune of loving gratitude every time they were aware of that awesome, silent Presence stirring within the depths of their souls and telling them of His Love.

Yes, they were grateful—grateful that God is God, Jesus saves, the Spirit sanctifies, and they were empty vessels constantly being filled with every good thing.

Paul, in an outburst of gratitude, said, "I never stop thanking God for all the graces you have received through Jesus Christ. I thank Him that you have been enriched in so many ways, especially in your teachers and preachers" (1 Cor. 1:4-5).

These Christians were grateful, not only for the gift of grace, but for the teachers and preachers who kept that grace growing in their souls by truth without error, and a witness to the power of the Spirit among them.

Humble hearts are grateful hearts, and both humility and gratitude belong to truth, the truth of God's Love and Mercy to poor, undeserving sinners. Because that very Love was given gratuitously on the part of God, they had to receive and accept that Love with gratitude—anything less would be an offense to God.

To take that Love for granted would be lukewarmness, to receive that Love without the realization of one's unworthiness would be pride, but to accept it without gratitude would be insolence.

The men and women who believed Jesus was Lord and experienced His love in their daily lives and His Spirit in their hearts, were grateful children of a Provident Father. When they began to take things for granted, they had only to look back and they would once more look to God with grateful hearts.

Thanksgiving became a way of life to them because they saw God in everything. Nothing just happened; nothing was mere coincidence or chance. Everything was a gift from a loving Father to each of them.

He planned their lives, and they thanked Him for every minute of it. Paul made it clear when he said, "You must live your whole life according to the Christ you have received.... You must be rooted in Him and built on Him, and held firm by the faith you have been taught, and full of thanksgiving" (Col. 2:6-7).

Paul classifies thanksgiving with Faith for only a grateful heart has the power to believe those invisible mysteries that make life a challenge, a mystery, an awesome expecting of something wonderful to come.

Man's heart tends to give credit to itself for every good thing, but the heart of a Christian realizes that to God alone goes the glory and the thanksgiving for talents, health, success, the pruning of the cross, and the glory of Heaven.

This spirit of thanksgiving gave them a kind of exhilarating freedom of mind. He took care of them—care of everything—and they thanked Him from the bottom of their hearts.

When crosses came their way, they thanked Him, and suddenly the crosses were easier to carry.

When joy was their portion, they thanked Him, and it seemed they tasted a little bit of Heaven.

When pain pierced their bodies through sickness or torture, they thanked Him and, like Stephen, they felt as if Heaven opened and God smiled upon them (Acts 7:56).

When their neighbor disappointed them, they thanked God for detaching them from the things and men of his world.

When their lives became a mystery, they thanked God that they were wrapped in His Arms as they faced the problems they could not solve.

When they were hated because of His Name, they sang hymns of thanksgiving because they knew their reward was great in Heaven.

And when they lost their possessions for the sake of the Kingdom, they thanked God because they were to roam God's earth, free of attachments, and free of things that tied them down and prevented them from finding Him.

Their thanksgiving turned to praise for praise was the music rising to Heaven from grateful hearts. The more gratitude they felt, the more praise they expressed. It never seemed enough when they said, "Thank You, Lord"; their love drove them on to say, "Praise God!"

To them, thanksgiving was an act of gratitude for something God did for them, but praise was to thank God for God—to look at His Beauty and praise His Omnipotence, to see His Mercy and praise His Goodness, and to feel His Love and praise His Compassion.

When they thanked Him for joy and sorrow, they praised the Wisdom that saw to their needs and gave them those things that increased their glory in the Kingdom.

When they thanked Him for the persecution that spread the Good News far and wide, they praised Him for manifesting the truth that the wisdom of man is foolishness to God.

When they thanked Him for sending Jesus to save them, their hearts rang out in songs of Praise for His Infinite Love and Mercy. It became sheer joy for them to Praise God, for it somehow made them selfless, at least for a moment.

There was something about praising God that was unlike any other prayer they said. It made the worst of them noble; the weakest, strong; and the most selfish, generous. It lifted them above themselves and made them think of God alone.

The more they praised Him, the more they found to praise. They began by praising Him for Jesus, for Faith, Hope, and Love, and for Redemption. One day they praised Him when they were being questioned, humiliated, and flogged in public, for the sake of His Name and when their hearts rang out in songs of Praise, an invisible force took hold of them, as at Pentecost and they danced for joy.

In the mind of Paul, God had chosen them to live holy and spotless lives through their love for Jesus. God had made them adopted sons, so they would "praise the glory of His grace" for all eternity (Eph. 1:4-6). It was Jesus Himself in them who would bear the fruit of goodness and make them pure and blameless as He prepared them to meet the Father face to face (Phil. 1:10-11).

It was through Jesus that these Christians offered praise to God because only Jesus could bear the fruit of humility in them. A man must step aside when he praises God. He must acknowledge that God is supreme, God alone is good and holy, and God is the giver of all gifts. Man's creation, life, and talents are all gifts from a loving God, without any merit on the part of the recipient. This attitude of humble gratitude is what makes Praise a sacrifice to God.

It is significant in the Gospel of St. Luke to see Zechariah receiving his power of speech from God and then praising God. We can be sure that this holy man was always grateful for the gift of speaking but only when that power was taken away and returned to him did he realize that the very Power of God was behind a gift that he, and many like him, took for granted.

We all thank God for the things He gives to us, and most of the time we do so because we are the recipients of either spiritual or temporal gifts but it is not often that we modern Christians praise God because He is so worthy of praise. Only an unselfish soul can praise God in pain, thank God in joy, and sing hymns of love in his heart for every moment he is allowed to live and breathe.

"Through Jesus," St. Paul told the Hebrews, "let us of-fer God an unending sacrifice of praise, a verbal sacrifice that is offered every time we acknowledge His Name" (Heb.

13:15). We don't often think of a sacrifice being "verbal," but when we must make a choice of speaking our own name or the Name of Jesus, of speaking of our life or His life, of our fruit or His fruit, of our works or His works, we readily see that praise can be and is a magnificent sacrifice that we can render to God.

If we love Him much, it will be a painless sacrifice, but if our love is lukewarm, then we shall find speaking of Jesus in preference to ourselves a painful sacrifice.

When we look at the life of John the Baptist, we see this form of Praise very evident. He acknowledged before crowds that he was not the Messiah, that there was One to come who was so holy he was not worthy to loosen His sandals, One who would baptize them with the Holy Spirit (John 1:19-34).

John the Baptist arrived at a most perfect form of praise when he said, "He must increase, but I must decrease" (John 3:30). This is real praise, not just the lip service of the Pharisee, who thanked God he was not like the rest of men and then proceeded to praise his own works and actions.

When John told the crowds that he was not worthy to loosen the sandal strap of the One who would follow him, he gave Jesus the highest praise. A proud person is incapable of praise, for he attributes everything to himself and self-praise is ever on his lips and in his heart.

The first Christian, however, desired nothing else but to speak of and praise Jesus. The more he praised God, the more he emptied himself until he slowly began to give glory to God in everything.

Praise rose from within the Christian, and God, seeing that spirit of love, would one day *return* that praise. Paul told his converts that it was not the letter of the law that made them pleasing to God; it was the spirit. "Real circumcision is in the heart," he told them, "something not of the letter but of the spirit. A Jew like that may not be praised by man, but he will be praised by God" (Rom. 2:28-29).

The Christian was not to court the praise of men nor judge their motives. It is a judging of motives that makes men either blame or praise other men. If the first Christian was to forget himself and spend his time in seeking God, this principle also applied to his neighbor. Only God knew the heart of man, and the Christian's only duty was to love his neighbor in the same way God loved him. He must leave judgment to God. Both blame or praise would come from the Searcher of all hearts.

"There must be no passing of premature judgment," Paul advised them. "Leave that until the Lord comes: He will light up all that is hidden in the dark, and reveal the secret intentions of men's hearts. Then will be the time for each one to have whatever praise he deserves from God" (1 Cor. 4:5).

They possessed the very words of Jesus to assure them of this truth. Jesus told the crowds that on the last day He would say to the elect—when He was hungry they gave Him to eat, gave Him drink when He was thirsty, and visited Him when He was sick. All of this is praise—praise from God Himself, who commends His faithful ones for being loyal. Only after He praises them to their utter amazement will He reward them with the Kingdom (Matt. 25:34-40).

The Beatitudes are forms of praise, for Jesus calls the faithful "blessed" when they are poor in spirit, gentle, chaste, peaceful, and pure of heart. What greater praise for any human being than to have God Himself, the Holy of Holies, call him "blessed" (Matt. 5:1-9)?

Yes, Jesus will praise His children, the fruit of His Redemption, in the presence of the Enemy and his followers. He will praise these inferior human beings in the presence of those superior intelligences whose pride forever prevents them from praising God. The Enemy shall be crushed to see weak men held in such high esteem by the Most High Lord, and the Wisdom of God will be manifest in a most marvelous way as He unfolds the secret holiness and sacrifices of His children. Truly, then they will all understand how wonderfully praiseworthy is God.

Prayer of Peaceful Serenity

The word "peace" meant more to the first Christians than the absence of war. In fact, their very fruit in Jesus created conditions conducive to war. Evil men who saw in the Christians a spirit of holiness were determined to eradicate them from the face of the earth. Their hatred for Jesus and His followers engendered persecutions and perpetrated cruelties that were insane and inhuman.

These Christians were under no illusions that being a Christian made all men love them or assured them of a place in this world. They lived in an atmosphere of the worst kind of war—the war between consciences, between ideals and goals, and between spirits. Jesus made it clear that He was a God of Peace but He would not bring peace. "Do not suppose," He said, "that I have come to bring peace to the earth: it is not peace I have come to bring but a sword. For I have come to set a man against his father, a daughter against her mother, a daughter-in-law against her mother-in-law. A man's enemies will be those of his own household" (Matt. 10:34-36).

The life Jesus required of His followers made dissension inevitable, for those requirements left no doubts and presented no alternatives. Every man from then on who had to make a choice would cause some kind of turmoil in the lives of others. The Son of God became man and showed us all how a child of God must live. With the force of His example behind His words, Jesus divided all mankind into groups and gave to each individual a choice to make — either for Him or against Him.

His love, mercy, and salvation would be extended to all, but He would never interfere with their free will. He offered peace to all, but many would not accept it because the peace He offered was born from within — a peace that rose from the ashes of interior violence in the heart of man.

The refusal of some to accept peace on His terms caused Jesus to shed tears of anguish. Scripture tells us that "as He drew near and came in sight of the city He shed tears over it and said, 'If you in your turn had only understood on this day the message of peace!'" (Luke 19:41-42).

It was not man-made peace that Jesus desired for His followers. That kind of peace was short-lived, for it was dependent upon the will and gratification of the strong. It always entailed the good of some to the detriment of others. No, the peace that Jesus desired for His friends was a gift—a gift from Himself—a gift that was part of Himself.

"Peace, I bequeath you," He told them, "my own peace I give you—a peace the world cannot give, this is my gift to you" (John 14:27). The only kind of peace the world can give is to determine who among its inhabitants is the strongest and most influential, and then those who are weaker stand aside until they become strong and the whole process of war begins again.

Greed and the desire for power is the seed that sprouts dissension and war. It is seldom that real injustice brings about a just war. The first Christian had to root out of his soul all greed and worldly ambition, and this is why the world was incapable of giving *him* peace, for the Christian removed from his soul both the cause of war and the false peace that comes from the absence of turmoil.

The source of peace for the Christian was and is Jesus. When Jesus told His Apostles they would be scandalized in

Him and each go his own way, He told them that He would not be alone, for the Father was with Him. Jesus had found His peace in the Father, and since He was always united to the Father and saw the Father in every situation He never lost His peace.

This was the secret of His peace: union with the Father. His peace was not of this world, and to make this clear He said to them, "I have told you all this so you may find peace in me. In the world you will have trouble but be brave: I have conquered the world" (John 16:33).

Jesus conquered the world by not permitting it to be the source of His peace. The world was not to determine when He had or did not have peace. His peace was a sure, ever flowing river, coming to Him from the Father. He wanted His followers to find their peace in Him just as He found His peace in the Father.

St. Paul told the Romans that Christ came "to bring the Good News of Peace" and that He was our "means of reconciliation with the Father." These Christians were to do everything in their power "to preserve the unity of the Spirit by the peace that bound them together" (Eph. 2:16; 4:3; Col. 1:18, 20).

To the writer of the Epistle to the Hebrews peace was an important part of the Christian's life. "Always be wanting peace with all people," he told them, "and the holiness without which no one can see the Lord. Be careful that no one is deprived of the grace of God and that no root of bitterness should begin to grow and make trouble" (Heb. 12:14-15).

Peace was the very foundation of the Christian life, for peace made them free of the rancor and bitterness that prevented them from loving their neighbor and deprived them of grace.

Peter explained to the Christians the need to seek peace when he said, "Remember, anyone who wants to have a happy life and to enjoy prosperity must banish malice from his tongue, deceitful conversation from his lips; he must never yield to evil but must practice good; he must seek peace and pursue it. Because the face of the Lord frowns on evil men but the eyes of the Lord are turned towards the virtuous" (1 Pet. 3:10-12).

The basis of Christian peace was virtue, the bearing of fruit, and since Jesus was the One who bore fruit in them, it was the peace of Jesus they possessed. Peace did not come easy; it was the fruit of the Divine Indwelling—the fruit of the Spirit of the Lord.

Peace was precious to the first Christians; they sought it not for itself but because it kept them open to receive the grace of Jesus into their souls and prepared them to enter the Kingdom. "While you are waiting," Peter told them, "do your best to live lives without spot or stain so that He will find you at peace" (2 Pet. 3:14).

Peace formed a part of every facet of their lives. Paul gave the Philippians a blueprint for peace, and it began with joy. He told them that he wanted them to be "happy, always happy in the Lord." He wanted them to be tolerant and never to worry. Most of all he desired that when they needed anything, they were to pray for it, "asking God for it with prayer and thanksgiving." It was in this attitude of mind that Paul promised them a wonderful effect from this childlike confidence. He told them, "That peace of God, which is so much greater than we can understand, will guard your hearts and your thoughts in Christ Jesus" (Phil. 4:4, 6-7).

We see then that joy in the Lord, tolerance without bitterness, freedom from worry, and confidence in the Father's Providence would obtain for them that peace that acted as a guard over their thoughts and hearts.

With this groundwork accomplished, he advised them to "fill their minds with everything that is true, everything that is noble, everything that is good and pure and everything that may be thought virtuous or worthy of praise" (Phil. 4:8).

The peace of the early Christian was a deep union with God as Father, Jesus as Lord, and the Spirit as Sanctifier. He raised his mind to the Father and drank in the realization that this great God was truly his Father.

He let the thought of the Fatherhood of God penetrate his soul until it rested in it like a child in its mother's arms — secure and unafraid. Power to withstand the trials of life accompanied this realization, for if "God was with them who could be against them?" (Rom. 8:31).

The Christian entered into the Spirit of Jesus and let His gentleness penetrate his soul. He not only thought of Jesus; he "put on His Mind." He let the gentle, merciful Jesus take over his life to the point where he thought like Him and loved like Him. He was not satisfied just to pray to Jesus; he let Jesus bear fruit in him by giving his entire life to Him. The peaceful Jesus lived in him, and he would eradicate everything in his life that prevented that peaceful, gentle Christ from radiating.

Living Prayer

The first Christian never tired of contemplating the mystery of his soul being a Temple of the Holy Spirit. He was very much aware that that Temple must not in any way be defiled. He would adorn it with the beauty of love, peace, joy, kindness, compassion, mercy, and self-control. He would sweep it clean if the mud of sin ever marred its beauty and most of all, the atmosphere surrounding that Temple would be one of peace. No turbulence was allowed to make its home there.

And when storms were inevitable, they closed the doors and windows of that Temple—their minds and hearts—and stayed close to the Guest of their souls, the Spirit of the Lord. They held their peace, for in that peace was a shield against the Enemy.

When they feared the future, they entered into His Providence and held their peace.

When they were angry and disappointed, they entered into His Gentleness and held their peace.

When they suffered pain and persecution, they entered into His Wisdom and held their peace.

When they sinned and felt abandoned, they entered into His Mercy and held their peace.

When death loomed before them, they thought of His promises and held their peace.

Their lives were to be so united to God's Will that nothing would disturb their peace. Every time Jesus appeared to His Apostles after the Resurrection He greeted them with, "Peace be with you!" It was as if He were constantly reminding them of the gift He bequeathed to them. His Resurrection was proof to them that He was truly God's Son and His Promises were true; the Hope He offered was sure; the Faith He inspired was real. All this was to assure their peace for it came from Him, the unchanging God, and nothing should disturb that peace.

The first time He appeared to His Apostles He questioned the motives for their disturbed souls. "Why are you so agitated," He asked, "and why are these doubts rising in your hearts?" (Luke 24:38). Agitation and doubts destroyed their peace, and their Master asked, "Why?" If they really believed everything He told them, then why were they disturbed?

We have sympathy for these Apostles, who witnessed such cruelties heaped upon their Master. We understand their doubts when the One in whom they put their hopes was suddenly snatched away from them and all seemed lost. Yes, we poor unenlightened human beings understand, but Jesus did not!

He had explained to them many times that it was necessary for Him to suffer and die but that He would rise on the third day. He was grateful for the love they exhibited for His pain and sorrow, but He did not understand why they were not anxiously waiting for His Resurrection.

If He rewarded them for visiting the sick, how much more would He reward them for being compassionate towards His Passion. Their compassion was not His complaint but the fact that their sorrow was selfish. It was mixed with a loss of Hope, with a realization that the worldly glory they thought was theirs was gone and that Jesus was not a military leader delivering them from tyranny. This kind of selfish sorrow completely obliterated from their minds the thought of His Resurrection, and as a result, doubts and agitation took away their peace.

It is the same with us as it was with the first Christians. We are human beings and we *feel* pain, sorrow, separation, and disappointment, but we cannot permit these trials to disturb our peace. Nothing must be permitted to take away our Hope in His Word, His Promises, and His Resurrection. In Him we possess our peace, in Him is our Hope, in Him is our Faith, and in Him is our heart.

He expects us to have such Faith that we can move the mountains of doubt that obstruct the view of His Face.

He expects us to have such Hope that no disappointment, heartache or pain discourages us.

He expects us to have such Love that we desire nothing in this world but His Holy Will.

He wills us to have such Peace that neither the Enemy, the world, nor our own selfish desires can disturb Its presence in our souls.

Peace is a gift we must ever pursue and, once we have found it, hold it fast for it is part of Him. With Him in us nothing is big enough, nothing is great enough, nothing is important enough for us to lose His Presence.

Peace and Presence go together. We may not *feel* His Presence, but His pruning Love will preserve our Peace.

We may have sorrow, but His Presence will hold fast our Peace.

Men of the world may hate us, but His Peace will prevent our souls from being warped by hatred.

We may be hungry, thirsty, without home or land, but His Peace will shelter our souls from the cold of discontent and bitterness.

We may be angry over injustice, but His Peace will give us patience to wait for His Justice to prevail.

We may be fools in the eyes of the world but His Peace will make us stand tall and unafraid.

To those in the world, Peace is the absence of war, the absence of failure, the absence of turmoil, the absence of pain, the absence of suffering, the absence of hunger and thirst, and the absence of injustice.

To those who know Jesus, Peace is His Presence in their souls *when* they fail, when they are in turmoil, when they suffer, when they are in pain, when they suffer injustice, and when ambitious men make war upon them.

To the world, Peace is an *absence* of disturbing things, but to the Christian it is the *Presence* of Jesus in their souls that raises them above things.

This is another reason why the Peace He offers cannot be given by the world, for one form of Peace is dependent upon a *Presence* and another upon an *absence*.

His Presence and His Peace are gifts to us and we must hold on to those gifts. Nothing can be preferred to them and nothing can disturb that union of mind and heart.

Peace was to the first Christians and will be to the Christians in the last days, an abiding Presence that makes them see God as Father, love when they are not loved in return, stand tall in persecution, discern the difference between good and evil, be detached from the things of this world, possess a spirit of prayer, and ever be aware of the Divine Indwelling.

It was this kind of Peace that the early Christian wished to everyone when he said, "Peace be to you" and "Peace to this house."

"To you all, then, who are God's beloved, called to be saints, may God our Father and the Lord Jesus Christ send you grace and Peace" (Rom. 1:7).

MOTHER'S PRAYERS

JOURNEY INTO PRAYER

Introduction

The need to give communal worship and praise to God is fulfilled on Sunday by our Mass; and our love for each other is strengthened by our reception of the Eucharist—the Sacrament of Love. The graces received through the Sacraments give witness to our neighbor of the living Presence of the Lord in our midst. The praying community that has worshipped the Lord and has received His Body and Blood on Sunday must sustain itself throughout the week by a mutual sharing, shown by the corporal and spiritual acts of love and the bearing of fruit mentioned in the fifth chapter of Galatians: Love, Joy, Peace, Patience, Kindness, Goodness, Trustfulness, Gentleness, Self-control.

The Spirit leads each one of us in diverse ways: some best express their worship and needs to the Father by formal prayers, such as Novenas, Scriptural Rosary, and the use of Prayer Books.

There are some who pray by Scripture study, where they can feed their souls with His Words.

Others again, pray best alone, both in the privacy of their own homes and in the secret recesses of their souls.

In these days of stress and change, many members of the praying parish community find comfort and peace of mind in coming together to express their needs and share their joys.

It is not important which way one is led to pray, for the best way to pray is the way one prays best. It is only important that each one in the praying community understands that his prayer is essential to the growth, development, and holiness of both Shepherd and flock, for, "we are members of one another" (Eph. 4:25). The diversity of gifts glorifies the Father; the mutual sharing of gifts enriches the Body of Christ; and the continual growth of these gifts, in whatever way one is led, gives witness to the Sanctifying Power of the Holy Spirit.

Through the Providence of God, the following prayer formats were composed—to help the praying community attain a closer relationship with God and neighbor—a relationship fed by the Sacraments and sustained through prayer. These formats can be used both in community and in private.

An Explanation

The Lord encouraged us to pray for our spiritual needs when He said, "Ask and you shall receive. Seek and you shall find. Knock and it shall be opened" (Matt. 7:7). The following steps are designed for the praying community to bring the People of God to these three levels of Prayer.

The first, consisting of three formats, is entitled, "Ask and you shall receive." It is a beginner's Program—when a soul realizes that something is lacking in his Christian life, and he begins to ask himself some questions, such as, "Does God love me?" "If so, what to do about it?"—and—"Can I love Him in return?"

The formats in this program are to answer these questions of the inquiring soul:

Format I: God loves me.

Format II: Repentance

Format III: Hope

The Formats are merely guidelines, and can be changed in theme, thoughts, Scripture passages, etc. The leader must pray for discernment to ascertain the needs of the group in choosing new themes and Scripture.

The second—"Seek and you shall find." This program of three formats is geared toward an active cooperation with the Spirit in arriving at a closer resemblance to Christ in our daily life. The soul finds God in love and seeks to be like Him in every facet of life. This is a "How" Program, both as to what God has done for the soul and what the soul does for God. Its three formats are therefore entitled:

Format I: My Relationship to Myself

Format II: My Relationship to My Family

Format III: My Relationship to My Neighbor

The third—"Knock and it shall be opened." This program of eight formats explains what a Christian received at Baptism—the Seven Gifts of the Holy Spirit. The soul must be aware of the potential it has for great sanctity. This grace was given to it by the Mercy of the Father, the Sacrifice of the Son, and the Love of the Holy Spirit.

There is also a "How" section for each Gift, putting emphasis on the tools (Gifts) we already possess and need to develop.

The last format leads the soul to a higher plane, with more Scripture, more reflection, the celebration of the Eucharist, and the witnessing of the fruit of the Seven Gifts of the Spirit in our lives.

How This Guide Can Be Used

These Journeys can be used in various ways:

- ❧ As meditations for private prayer
- ❧ As family prayer
- ❧ As home retreats
- ❧ As a program of spiritual growth
- ❧ As formats for Beginner, Intermediate, and Advanced Praying Communities

Part I: "Ask and You Shall Receive"

GOD'S LOVE

Prayer—as a Realization of God's Love for Me.

The word "Prayer" means many things to many people. To some it means asking for "things"—for health, for success. To others, it means repentance, imploring God's Mercy for their sins and infidelities. Prayer is Praise and Thanksgiving to many. And to the majority of people it is a cry in times of distress.

Prayer is all of these things, but it is more. It is a Union of Love: God's Love and your love; it is an awareness of God's love for you—His personal love. To understand this love, reflect a few moments on the following thoughts (a few moments' pause after each thought):

- God loves me as if no one else existed.
- His love for me is beyond description.
- He knew me and loved me before He created anything.
- I am important to God; therefore, He sent His Son to live and die for me.
- He made me His dwelling place on earth at Baptism.
- He nourishes my soul with His own Body and Blood in the Eucharist.
- God dwells in me and longingly waits for my expressions of love.

Scripture Readings

Close your eyes and realize that the Father is speaking directly to you.

I have loved you with an everlasting love; so I am constant in My affection for you. (Jer. 31:3)

Before I formed you in the womb I knew you; before you came to birth I consecrated you....

Do not be afraid,
for I am with you to protect you. (Jer. 1:5, 8)

Does a woman forget her baby at the breast, or fail to
    cherish the son of her womb?
Yet even if these forget
I will never forget you.
See, I have branded you on the palms of My hands,
Your walls are always under My eyes. (Isa. 49:15-16)

I have chosen you;
stop being anxious and watchful, for I am your God.
I give you strength, I bring you help,
I uphold you with my victorious right hand.
Yes, all those who raged against you
shall be put to shame and confusion;
they who fought against you
shall be destroyed, and perish.
I am your God,
I am holding you by the right hand;
I tell you: Do not be afraid,
I will help you. (Isa. 41:10-13)

Do not be afraid, for I have redeemed you;
I have called you by your name — you are mine.
Should you pass through the sea, I will be with you;
or through rivers, they will not swallow you up.
Should you walk through fire, you will not be
scorched and the flames will not burn you.
For I am your God. (Isa. 43:1-3)

In your old age I shall still be the same;
When your hair is gray I shall still support you.
I have already done so, I have carried you,
I shall still support and deliver you. (Isa. 46:4)

My delight is to be with the children of men. (Prov.
8:31)

*Teaching and/or sharing of thoughts and manifestation
of God's Love in each other's life (for those who wish to
do so). Although sharing is not necessary, it is a great
help to others to see examples of how God
works in their personal lives.*

Song — relating to God's Love

REPENTANCE

As I begin to realize God's tremendous love, I feel a need to return that love—a desire to be washed clean of everything within me that is not like God. I look at the perfect image of the Father, Christ, and realize I am not like Him. The resemblance is faint and I want it to be more perfect.

What do I do—what stands in the way of my becoming another Christ? Christ is within me, waiting for me to let Him shine forth. What dark clouds stand between Christ and me, preventing my neighbor from seeing God's Son?

For a few moments let us compare ourselves with Christ.

I am proud; I attribute everything I do to myself—my talents, my success, my works, *but* Jesus gave credit to the Father for all His work. He said, "The Son can do nothing by Himself" (John 5:19), *so* I will radiate Christ by acknowledging all the good in me as coming from Jesus (*pause*).

I am critical; I find fault with my neighbor, misjudging his motives, *but* Jesus said, "If there is one of you who has not sinned, let him be the first to throw a stone" (John 8:7) and "Father, forgive them; they do not know what they are doing"

(Luke 23:34), *so* I will radiate Christ by making a real effort to see good in my neighbor, and loving him as he is (*pause*).

I am impatient; I get angry when things do not go my way, *but* Jesus was patient with the faults of the Apostles, the pressure of the crowds, and the hatred of His enemies, *so* I will radiate Christ by being compassionate with the faults of others and calm in disturbing situations, seeing an opportunity to imitate Christ (*pause*).

I am ambitious: I do not care how many people I hurt to arrive at success, *but* Jesus said, "Set your hearts on His Kingdom and these other things will be given you as well" (Luke 12:31), *so* I will radiate Christ by using my talents to the best of my ability — to extend the Kingdom and obtain the good of my neighbor (*pause*).

I am fearful: I fear death, loneliness, sickness, failure, and the future, *but* Jesus said, "Do not let your hearts be troubled" (John 14:1) and "I am going now to prepare a place for you" (John 14:2) and "Come to Me ... and I will give you rest" (Matt. 11:28), *so* I will radiate Christ by acting upon His Word, and having assurance He will take care of me (*pause*).

I find it hard to forgive and forget, *but* Jesus said, "If you forgive others their failings, your Heavenly Father will forgive you yours, but if you do not forgive others, your Father will not forgive you your failings either" (Matt. 6:14-15), *so* I will radiate Christ by being the first to forgive, and showing by some gesture of reconciliation I have forgotten (*pause*).

Reflection

You have just compared your actions with the actions of Jesus. Now for a few moments, give the Spirit the opportunity to take away your inner burdens and disturbing memories, those feelings that keep you from fully radiating Christ. Close your eyes and take Jesus by the hand. Look at whatever disturbs you, but look at it through the eyes of Jesus. See with His eyes; love with His Heart; and forgive with His Mercy.

My Jesus, there have been many hurts in my life, and I feel them still. Melt them away with Your love — so I won't hurt anymore. I put my hand in Yours and I feel secure and unafraid.

Scripture Readings

Come now, let us talk this over, says God.
Though your sins are like scarlet, they
shall be as white as snow; though they are
red as crimson, they shall be like wool. (Isa. 1:18)

I myself taught them to walk;
I took them in my arms;
Yet they have not understood that I was the one
    looking after them.
I led them with reins of kindness,
With leading-strings of love.
I was like someone who lifts an infant close against
    his cheek;
Stooping down to him I gave him his food.
How could I part with you?
How could I give you up?
My heart recoils from it—
My whole being trembles at the thought. (Osee
    [Hosea] 11:3-4, 8)

I have dispelled your faults like a cloud, your sins
    like a mist.
Come back to me, for I have redeemed you.
    (Isa. 44:22)

They had left in tears,
I will comfort them as I lead them back;
I will guide them to streams of water,

by a smooth path where they will not stumble.
Their soul will be like a watered garden,
they will sorrow no more.
I will change their mourning into gladness,
comfort them, give them joy after their troubles,
refresh my priests with rich food,
and see my people have their fill of my good things.
Stop your weeping,
Dry your eyes,
Your hardships will be redressed. (Jer. 31:9, 12,
     13, 16)

I did forget you for a brief moment,
but with great love will I take you back.
In excess of anger, for a moment
I hid my face from you.
But with everlasting love I have taken pity on you,
says God, your Redeemer. (Isa. 54:7-8)

> *Teaching and/or sharing of thoughts, or*
> *witnessing to God's Mercy in your life.*
>
> *Song*

Hope

In Heaven we will see God face to face — so faith falls away. In Heaven we will possess God — so hope falls away. In Heaven we will love God as He loves Himself — so love remains. Faith, Hope, and Love on earth — and Vision, Possession, and Union with God in Heaven — are not two separate lives we live, but merely two stages of the same life.

On earth we are given Faith — to see God *now*. On earth we are given Hope — to possess God *now*. On earth we are given Love — to grow in union with God *now*. The Kingdom of Heaven begins *now* — and varies only in degree.

Reflect a few moments on each of the following thoughts:

- The Blessed Trinity made their home in me at Baptism and I must realize their Presence.
- Through the Gifts of the Holy Spirit, received in Confirmation, I was given the power to witness, by holiness of life, to His Presence among us.
- I must accept the healing power of Penance, the Sacrament of Reconciliation, as ointment for deeprooted faults.

- Am I conscious of the Abiding Presence of Jesus in my soul after the Sacred Species of the Eucharist is gone?
- I must listen as God speaks to my soul through good thoughts, inspirations, and intuitions.
- I have been chosen by God to become a Saint; this is His Will.
- I am destined to be eternally happy. I shall begin now —for all of Heaven lives in me.

Scripture Readings

We, with our unveiled faces reflecting like mirrors the brightness of the Lord, all grow brighter and brighter as we are turned into the image that we reflect; this is the work of the Lord who is Spirit. (2 Cor. 3:18)

We are only earthenware jars that hold this treasure —to make it clear that such an overwhelming power comes from God, and not from us. (2 Cor. 4:7)

May He enlighten the eyes of your mind so you can see what hope His call holds for you, what rich glories He has promised the saints will inherit, and how infinitely great is the power that He has exercised for us believers. (Eph. 1:18-19)

Out of His infinite Glory, may He give you the power, through His Spirit, for your hidden self to grow strong, so that Christ may live in your hearts through Faith, and then planted in Love and built on Love you will, with all the Saints, have the strength to grasp the breadth and the length, the height and the depth of His Love. (Eph. 3:16-18)

Then I heard a loud voice call from the Throne, "You see this city? Here God lives among men. He will make His home among them; they shall be His people, and He will be their God; His Name is God-with-them. He will wipe away all tears from their eyes; there will be no more death and no more mourning or sadness. The world of the past is gone." (Rev. 21:3-4)

Be happy at all times; pray constantly; and for all things give thanks to God.... May the God of peace make you perfect and holy; and may you all be kept safe and blameless, spirit, soul and body, for the coming of Our

Lord Jesus Christ. God has called you and He will not fail you (1 Thess. 5:16-18, 23-24).

> *Teaching on Hope — and/or sharing ideas on preserving Joy of Heart.*

> *Song*

✿

Part II: "Seek and You Shall Find"

Psalm or any Song

MY RELATIONSHIP TO MYSELF

Consideration

If I am to love my neighbor as myself, I must first arrive at an understanding of my own dignity: my soul is immortal, it was created to the image and likeness of God, it was redeemed by the life and death of God's Son, and, through grace, it is the dwelling place of the Trinity. I am a child of God, destined for Eternal Glory; therefore, I am important to God because of all He has done for me.

Silent reflection on the above consider-
ation (approximately five minutes)

Litany

Leader: For creating my soul to Your image and
likeness—

People: I thank you, O my God.

Leader: For watching over me as a mother her only
child—

People: I thank you, O my God.

Leader: For keeping me in existence—

People: I thank you, O my God.

Leader: For giving me the treasures of nature for my
enjoyment—

People: I thank you, O my God.

Leader: For loving me enough to prune me—

People: I thank you, O my God.

Leader: For giving me Your living Presence in the
Sacraments—

People: I thank you, O my God.

Those who wish may add their own invocations,
to which the refrain is repeated by the people.

Journey into Prayer

Meditation: Baptism

At Baptism I received grace—that quality that makes me share in the very nature of God. If I could see a soul clothed with grace, it would be a thing of such beauty and splendor that I would think it was God. I am made holy with the very holiness of God. I am never alone for I always possess within me the Three Divine Persons, who abide with me and live in me.

My duty to myself consists in strengthening my Faith by a daily effort to become more aware of this Divine Indwelling; in a greater assurance (Hope) that Jesus in me will bear fruit in plenty; and in a deeper understanding of the transforming Love of the Holy Spirit.

Silent Reflection (approximately five minutes)

Sharing of ideas on how we can better reflect Christ in our daily lives

Scripture Readings

I saw you struggling in your blood as I was passing, and I said to you: Live, and grow like the grass of the field. You developed and grew but you were quite naked. Then I saw you as I was passing. Your time had come — the time for love. I spread part of My cloak over you [chosen] and covered your nakedness; I bound myself by oath, I made a covenant with you [supernatural life through Baptism]; it is the Lord God who speaks, and you were mine. I bathed you in water, I washed the blood off you, I anointed you with oil [Confirmation], I gave you embroidered dresses [Grace], fine leather shoes, a linen headband, and a cloak of silk. I loaded you with jewels [Gifts of the Holy Spirit], gave you bracelets for your wrists and a necklace for your throat. I put a beautiful diadem on your head. You were more and more beautiful because I had clothed you with My own splendor. (Ezekiel 16:6-14)

Think of the love that the Father has lavished on us, by letting us be called God's children; and that is what we are. (1 John 3:1)

The proof that you are sons is that God has sent the Spirit of His Son into our hearts: the Spirit that cries, "Abba, Father," and it is this that makes you a son; you are not a slave anymore; and if God has made you son, then He has made you heir. (Gal. 4:6-7)

Journey into Prayer

Discussion on Scriptural Readings

Renewal of Baptismal Vows

I, N., who through the tender mercy of the Eternal Father was privileged to be baptized "in the name of the Lord Jesus" (Acts 19:5), and thus to share in the dignity of His Divine Sonship, wish now, in the presence of this same loving Father and of His only begotten Son, to renew in all sincerity the promises I solemnly made at the time of my holy Baptism.

I, therefore, now do again renounce Satan. I renounce all his works; I renounce all his allurements.

Song

MY RELATIONSHIP TO MY FAMILY

Psalm or Song

Consideration

When Christ took upon Himself our human nature, He became flesh of our flesh, bone of our bone—and so it is in the

Family. Each member of the family belongs in a special way to the other members—and to Christ. My relationship to my family must be one of love and humble obedience. I must give myself generously and totally, without sparing and without reserve.

God has given me a special mission to my Family, which I alone can fulfill. I must encourage, uphold, forbear, excuse, love, and "be among them as one who serves." I cannot bring Christ to my neighbor and to the world if I have not first given Him to my Family.

Silent Reflection on Ways of Radiating Christ to My Family

Litany

Leader: That I may appreciate what the members of my family do for me

People: Lord, show me the way.

Leader: That I may excuse, overlook, or correct, as my duty demands

People: Lord, show me the way.

Leader: That I may be a joy and consolation to my loved ones

People: Lord, show me the way.

Leader: That I may be compassionate and helpful in
    times of sickness and crisis

People: Lord, show me the way.

Leader: That I may be an obedient, humble, and
    responsible member of my family

People: Lord, show me the way.

> *Additional invocations may be added spontane-*
> *ously and the refrain answered by all the members.*

Song

Meditation

God has destined from all Eternity that I belong to the family in which He has placed me. I need them and they need
me. Each one of us helps the others to become holy, and
thus fulfill our eternal destiny. I must realize that the differences in temperament, opinions, and personalities between
us present opportunities to fashion and develop my character
by the way in which I use them. I owe my family my loyalty,
devotion, and prayer, that we may together attain the fullness of Christ.

Silent Reflection (approximately five minutes)

Sharing ideas on better Family relations

Scripture Readings

Give way to one another in obedience to Christ. Wives should regard their husbands as they regard the Lord, since as Christ is head of the Church and saves the whole body, so is a husband the head of his wife; and as the Church submits to Christ, so should wives to their husbands, in everything. Husbands should love their wives just as Christ loved the Church and sacrificed Himself for her to make her holy. He made her clean by washing her in water with a form of words, so that when He took her to Himself she would be glorious, with no speck or wrinkle or anything like that, but holy and faultless....

Children, be obedient to your parents in the Lord —that is your duty. The first Commandment that has a promise attached to it is: "Honor your father and mother," and the promise is: "and you will prosper and have a long life in the Land." And, parents, never drive your children to resentment, but in bringing them up correct them and guide them as the Lord does. (Eph. 5:21-6:4)

Renewal of Family Commitment

Lord, God and Father, I take this Family that You have given me as my very own, to have and to hold, in sickness and in health, for richer or poorer, for better or worse. I promise to love, honor, and cherish them as precious gifts from Your hands. Teach us to grow together in holiness of life that we may some-day come together to share in Your Glory.

Song

✿

MY RELATIONSHIP WITH MY NEIGHBOR

Psalm or Song

Consideration

Christ has said, "I am the Vine, you are the branches" (John 15:5). Through Baptism, each one of us is a living branch, and all of us receive our life from the same source—Christ; we belong to one another in a spiritual union that is profound and mysterious—a union greater than any human ties, because the bond that unites us is the Holy Spirit, Who diffuses His Grace and Gifts to each member through Christ.

Let us imagine for a few moments a beautiful tree. It is a spiritual tree but similar in every way to a natural tree. The roots of this tree are sunk very deep into the soil of humility; these roots that shoot out in various directions are the many acts of Faith and Hope in your life. The trunk of this tree is Christ, and you are grafted by the Father to this trunk and you become a living branch.

This tree is nourished and fed by the Holy Spirit through the Sacraments, especially the Eucharist and the Sacrament of Reconciliation, and through virtues and good works. Each branch is fed by the same food, and each branch bears fruit in proportion as it takes in the life-giving nourishment. The roots, trunk, branches, and fruit all need one another and help make the tree beautiful for the Father to behold.

Silent Reflection (approximately five minutes)

Litany

Leader: That I may realize the dignity of my neighbor
People: Lord, that I may see.

Leader: That I may be more aware of the invisible
   Realities
People: Lord, that I may see.
Leader: That I may be more conscious of your need of
   me in the Church
People: Lord, that I may see.
Leader: That I may penetrate the mystery of Your
   Love in the Sacraments
People: Lord, that I may see.
Leader: That I may have the courage to commit my-
   self totally to the workings of Your Spirit
People: Lord, that I may see.

*Personal invocations for light may be
added, with everyone responding.*

Song

Sharing of Thoughts on Our Relationship to Each Other

Meditation
"A new Commandment I give you—that you love one another as I love you" (John 13:34).

It is easy to keep this Commandment if I realize that the same life-giving principle runs through each of us, and we are bound together in Christ through the Love of the Holy Spirit — living, growing, and developing together.

Thoughts that may help me to develop a deeper love for my neighbor:

- If I cannot excuse his actions, let me at least not judge his motives.
- I must endure the faults of others calmly and kindly taking into account the beam in my own eye.
- I will try to discover the good in my neighbor even though it may be eclipsed by many faults.
- I must persevere in doing good even in the face of ingratitude.
- I will adapt myself to the mentalities, preferences, and needs of my neighbor and acquire the habit of listening. In imitation of Christ, I will sacrifice myself generously for the good of others.
- When anyone arouses my anger, I will immediately pray for them and regain my peace of soul.

Song

Journey into Prayer

Sharing and/or spontaneous Prayer

Scripture Readings

You are God's chosen race, His saints; He loves you and you should be clothed in sincere compassion, in kindness and humility, gentleness and patience. Bear with one another, forgive each other as soon as a quarrel begins. The Lord has forgiven you; now you must do the same. Over all these clothes—to keep them together and complete them—put on Love. And may the Peace of Christ reign in your hearts, because it is for this that you were called together as parts of one Body. Always be thankful. Let the message of Christ, in all its richness, find a home within you. Teach each other, and advise each other, in all Wisdom. With gratitude in your hearts, sing psalms and hymns and inspired songs to God, and never do or say anything except in the Name of the Lord Jesus, giving thanks to God the Father through Him. (Col. 3:12-17)

We appeal to you, my brothers, to be considerate to those who are working among you and are above you in the Lord as your teachers. Have the greatest respect and affection for them because of their work. Be at peace among yourselves. And this is what we ask you to do, brothers: warn the idler, give courage to those who are apprehensive, care for the weak, and be patient with everyone. Make sure that people do not try to take revenge; you must all think of what is best for each other and for the community. Be happy at all times; pray constantly: and for all things give thanks to God because this is what God expects you to do in Christ Jesus. (1 Thess. 5:12-18)

Accepting the Anointing of my Confirmation
I, N., accept the power of the Holy Spirit, whose seal I received at my Confirmation. I desire to joyfully bear witness before men to the Suffering, Death, and Resurrection of our Lord Jesus Christ. I will try to reflect by holiness of life the Goodness of Christ and the Power of His Spirit.
Leader: The Spirit of Wisdom and Understanding
Response: I accept.
Leader: The Spirit of Right Judgment and Courage
Response: I accept.

Journey into Prayer

Leader: The Spirit of Knowledge and Love
Response: I accept.
Leader: The Spirit of Reverence in Your Service
Response: I accept.

Songs to the Holy Spirit

Part III: *"Knock and It Shall Be Opened"*

The Gifts received at Baptism and
strengthened at Confirmation

GIFT OF REVERENCE IN YOUR SERVICE
AND FEAR OF THE LORD

Leader: Alleluia! Alleluia!

Joyous Song

Scripture Readings

And the Spirit of the Lord shall rest upon him: the Spirit
of Wisdom, and of Understanding, the Spirit of Counsel,

and of Fortitude, the Spirit of Knowledge, and of Godliness. And he shall be filled with the Spirit of Fear of the Lord. (Isa. 11:2-3)

These are the very things that God has revealed to us through the Spirit, for the Spirit reaches the depths of everything, even the depths of God. After all, the depths of a man can only be known by his own spirit, not by any other man, and in the same way the depths of God can only be known by the Spirit of God. Now instead of the spirit of the world, we have received the Spirit that comes from God, to teach us to understand the Gifts that He has given us. Therefore, we teach, not in the way in which philosophy is taught, but in the way that the Spirit teaches us: we teach spiritual things spiritually. An unspiritual person is one who does not accept anything of the Spirit of God: he sees it all as nonsense; it is beyond his understanding because it can only be understood by means of the Spirit. A spiritual man, on the other hand, is able to judge the value of everything, and his own value is not to be judged by other men. As Scripture says: "Who can know the mind

of the Lord, so who can teach him?" But we are those
who have the mind of Christ (1 Cor. 2:10-16).

Silent reflection

Prayer: My Father, I thank You for giving me the Gift
of the Spirit of Reverence in Your Service (Fear of the
Lord).

Explanation of my Gift

Without this Gift I would never dream of calling God "my Father." Instead of representing God as a strong judge, the Holy
Spirit, through this Gift, shows me God as a most loving Father,
seeking only my good and showering me with His favors, affection, and mercy. This gives me a hatred for sin because sin
separates me from such a Father.

All together: By the Power of Your Word I am assured
that I possess this Gift of Reverence in Your service.

Silent Reflection

Song

How I cooperate with the Spirit

Blessed are the poor in spirit.

Fruit of the Spirit: self-control

Virtue of Hope and Temperance

I must grow in this Gift by being poor in spirit, watching over my heart that it does not become attached to "things." I will exercise self-control by being temperate and not going to excess in anything. Although this Gift causes me to throw myself into the arms of my Heavenly Father with confidence, I must ever be aware of His Infinite Majesty.

People: Mary, daughter of the Eternal Father, Mother of the Eternal Son, and Spouse of the Holy Spirit, intercede for us.

Silent Reflection

Teaching and Sharing of how best to grow in your situation—and/or spontaneous prayer

Song

GIFT OF FORTITUDE AND COURAGE

Leader: Alleluia! Alleluia!

Joyous Song

Scripture Readings

But you will receive power when the Holy Spirit comes on you, and then you will be My witnesses not only in Jerusalem but throughout Judea and Samaria, and indeed to the ends of the earth. (Acts 1:8)

Happy those who are persecuted in the cause of right: theirs is the Kingdom of Heaven. (Matt. 5:10)

[God] gives strength to the wearied,
He strengthens the powerless.
Young men may grow tired and weary,
youths may stumble,
but those who hope in God renew their strength,
they put on wings like eagles.
They run and do not grow weary,
walk and never tire. (Isa. 40:29-31)

Silent Reflection

Prayer: My Father, I thank You for giving me the Gift of Courage (Fortitude).

Explanation of my Gift

This Gift gives me courage to remain faithful to God's Law, the duties of my state in life, and to endure patiently the many difficulties and hardships that cross my path. It strengthens me to persevere in following the inspirations of the Holy Spirit, and to face the future without fear.

All together: By the Power of Your Word I am assured that I possess the Gift of Courage.

Silent Reflection

Song

Blessed are they who hunger and thirst after Justice.

Fruit of the Spirit: Joy

Virtue of Fortitude

How I cooperate with the Spirit
I will grow in this Gift by following the longing in my soul for holiness and union with God. I will quench my thirst for God's Kingdom on earth by spending myself for the good of others. The Will of God will be my

food, and I will show to others the sheer joy of soul that is the fruit of prayer and following the Spirit.

People: Mary, Daughter of the Eternal Father, Mother of the Eternal Son, and Spouse of the Holy Spirit, intercede for us.

Silent Reflection

Teaching and Sharing ideas and experiences — and/or spontaneous prayer

Song

GIFT OF PIETY AND LOVE

Leader: Alleluia! Alleluia!

Joyous Song

Scripture Readings

The proof that you are sons is that God has sent the Spirit of His Son into our hearts: the Spirit that cries, "Abba, Father," and it is this that makes you a son; you are not a slave any more; and if God has made you son, then He has made you heir. (Gal. 4:6-7)

The Spirit Himself and our Spirit bear united witness that we are children of God. And if we are children, we are heirs as well; heirs of God and co-heirs with Christ, sharing His sufferings so as to share His glory. (Rom. 8:16-17)

Before the world was made, He chose us, chose us in Christ, to be holy and spotless, and to live through love in His Presence, determining that we should become His adopted sons, through Jesus Christ, for His own kind purposes, to make us praise the glory of His grace, His free gift to us in the Beloved. (Eph. 1:4-6)

Shoulder My yoke and learn from Me, for I am gentle and humble in heart, and you will find rest for your souls. Yes, My yoke is easy and My burden light. (Matt. 11:29-30)

Prayer: My Father, I thank You for giving me the Gift of Love (Piety).

Explanation of my Gift

This Gift gives me a realization that I am a son of God, and this truth becomes a living, personal experience, transforming my prayer into childlike heart-to-heart talks with God. This Gift also smooths over differences and helps me overcome feelings of reserve and coldness toward my neighbor.

All together: By the Power of Your Word, I am assured that I possess this Gift of Love.

Silent Reflection

Song

Blessed are the meek.

Fruit of the Spirit: Gentleness

How I cooperate with the Spirit

I must grow in this Gift by making every effort to be meek and gentle during the many trials, contradictions, and humiliations in daily life. I will bring to mind that these painful experiences are necessary for me to realize my insufficiency and need of God's help. With this Gift I can control all interior feelings of antipathy, anger, and resentment, and treat everyone as a brother because we have the same Father.

People: Mary, Daughter of the Eternal Father, Mother of the Eternal Son, and Spouse of the Holy Spirit, intercede for us.

Silent Reflection

Teaching and Sharing of ideas on how to show love by being meek and gentle — and/or spontaneous prayer

Song

GIFT OF COUNSEL AND RIGHT JUDGMENT
Leader: Alleluia! Alleluia!

Festive Song

Scripture Readings
The Advocate, the Holy Spirit, whom the Father will send in My Name, will teach you everything, and

remind you of all I have said to you. Peace I bequeath to you, My own peace I give you, a peace the world cannot give, this is My gift to you. (John 14:26-27)

Speak, Lord, Your servant is listening. (1 Sam. 3:9)

I shall ask the Father, and He will give you another Advocate to be with you forever, that Spirit of Truth whom the world can never receive since it neither sees Him or knows Him—but you know Him, because He is with you; He is in you. (John 14:16-17)

Silent Reflection

Prayer: My Father, I thank You for giving me the Spirit of Right Judgment (Counsel).

Explanation of my Gift

This Gift gives me the ability to recall the words and example of Jesus, and apply them to the circumstances of daily life. It enables me to understand the voice of the Spirit as He directs me in the way of holiness. It makes me seek His light and guidance in all decisions, especially those that affect others. It makes me realize my own misery and thereby compassionate with the miseries of others. I realize that all I have is a gift from God.

All together: By the Power of Your Word, I am assured that I possess this Gift of Right Judgment.

Silent Reflection

Song

Blessed are the merciful.

Fruit of the Spirit: Goodness

How I cooperate with the Spirit

I must grow in this Gift by being merciful, realizing that as God stoops to my misery and forgives, I, too, must forgive others. I will be careful not to be obstinate and attached to my own opinions so that I can make the right decisions, seeking always the good of others.

People: Mary, Daughter of the Eternal Father, Mother of the Eternal Son, and Spouse of the Holy Spirit, intercede for us.

Silent Reflection

Journey into Prayer

*Teaching and Sharing of ideas and
thoughts — spontaneous prayer if desired*

Song

GIFT OF KNOWLEDGE
Leader: Alleluia! Alleluia!

Festive Song

Scripture Readings

What gain, then, is it for a man to win the whole world and ruin his life? And, indeed, what can a man offer in exchange for his life? For if anyone in this adulterous and sinful generation is ashamed of Me and of My Words, the Son of Man will also be ashamed of him when he comes in the glory of His Father with the holy angels. (Mark 8:36-38)

Martha, Martha, you worry and fret about so many things, and yet few are needed, indeed only one. It is

Mary who has chosen the better part; it is not to be taken from her. (Luke 10:41-42)

Vanity of vanities. All is vanity! (Eccles. 1:1)

Know this: God works wonders for those He loves; God hears me when I call to Him. (Ps. 4:3)

It is the same God that said, "Let there be light shining out of darkness," who has shone in our minds to radiate the light of the knowledge of God's glory, the glory on the face of Christ. (2 Cor. 4:6)

Silent Reflection

Prayer: My Father, I thank You for giving me the Gift of the Spirit of Knowledge.

Aids the Theological Virtue of Hope	*Explanation of my Gift* This Gift gives me the realization of the one thing necessary and a compassionate detachment from all things. It gives me the ability to see the reflection of God in all His creation, praise Him for it, but ever

remember that all things are passing. Knowledge also increases my Hope, enabling me to see God in every situation — pleasant and unpleasant — knowing that all things tend to good for those who love God.

All together: By the Power of Your Word, I am assured that I possess this Gift of Knowledge.

Silent Reflection

Song

Blessed are they who mourn.

Fruit of the Spirit: Patience

How I cooperate with the Spirit
I must grow in this Gift by lovingly embracing the sufferings of life and seeing in them the Glory to come. I will use the Sacrament of Reconciliation as a means of expressing my repentant love. I will exhibit more patience with myself and with my neighbor.

People: Mary, Daughter of the Eternal Father, Mother of the Eternal Son, Spouse of the Holy Spirit, intercede for us.

Silent Reflection

Teaching and Sharing—and/or spontaneous prayer

Song

GIFT OF UNDERSTANDING
Leader: Alleluia! Alleluia!

Festive Song

Scripture Readings

Ever since God created the world, His everlasting Power and Deity, however invisible, have been there for the mind to see in the things He has made. (Rom. 1:20)

If you do not believe Me when I speak about things in this world, how are you going to believe Me when I speak to you about heavenly things? (John 3:12)

The Good News which has reached you is spreading all over the world and producing the same results as it has among you ever since the day when you heard about God's grace and understood what this really is. (Col. 1:6)

That will explain why, ever since the day He told us, we have never failed to pray for you, and what we ask God is that through perfect Wisdom and spiritual understanding you should reach the fullest Knowledge of His Will. So you will be able to lead the kind of life which the Lord expects of you, a life acceptable to Him in all its aspects; showing the results in all the good actions you do and increasing your knowledge of God. You will have in you the strength, based on His own glorious Power, never to give in, but to bear anything joyfully, thanking the Father who has made it possible for you to join the saints and with them to inherit the light. Because that is what He has done: He has taken us out of the power of darkness and created a place for us in the Kingdom of the Son that He loves, and in Him, we gain our freedom, the forgiveness of our sins. (Col. 1:9-14)

Silent Reflection

Prayer: My Father, I thank You for giving me the Gift of the Spirit of Understanding.

Aids the Theological Virtue of Faith	*Explanation of my Gift* This Gift gives me light and intuitions regarding Divine Mysteries. With Faith I believe the revelations God has given me, and with the Gift of Understanding I "see" the inner sense of these mysteries. It raises me above reasoning in prayer, and helps me, with a simple gaze, to penetrate the Divine Mysteries.

All together: By the Power of Your Word, I am assured that I possess this Gift of Understanding.

Silent Reflection

Song

Blessed are the clean of heart.

Fruit of the Spirit: Trustfulness

How I cooperate with the Spirit

I must grow in this Gift by preparing myself with great purity of heart. I will be careful not to measure Divine things by worldly standards, interpreting them according to my personal views, and being careful not to be swayed by half-truths. I will develop the ability to listen, knowing that God often enkindles light by the clash of ideas.

People: Mary, Daughter of the Eternal Father, Mother of the Eternal Son, and Spouse of the Holy Spirit, intercede for us.

Silent Reflection

Teaching and Sharing—and/or spontaneous prayer

Song

GIFT OF WISDOM
Leader: Alleluia! Alleluia!

Festive Song

Scripture Readings

How good God is—only taste and see!
Happy the man who takes shelter in Him! (Ps. 34:8)

But anyone who is joined to the Lord is one spirit with Him. (1 Cor. 6:17)

How rich are the depths of God, how deep His Wisdom and Knowledge, and how impossible to penetrate His motives or understand His methods! (Rom. 11:33)

I bless You, Father of heaven and of earth, for hiding these things from the learned and the clever and revealing them to mere children. (Matt. 11:25)

Since you have been brought to true life with Christ, you must look for the things that are in heaven, where Christ is, sitting at God's right hand. (Col. 3:1)

We can know that we are living in Him and He is living in us because He lets us share His Spirit. (1 John 4:13)

May the God our Lord Jesus Christ, the Father of glory, give you a spirit of Wisdom and perception of what is revealed, to bring you to full knowledge of Him. (Eph. 1:17)

Silent Reflection

Prayer: My Father, I thank You for giving me the Gift of the Spirit of Wisdom.

Aids the Theological Virtue of Love

Explanation of my Gift

As the Gift of Understanding makes me "see" the Lord, the Gift of Wisdom makes me "taste" how sweet He is. It gives me a strong Love, ready to experience consolation or desolation with equal peace of soul. As there is an affinity of thought and affection between mother and child, so, through this Gift, I have an affinity of thought and affection with the Father.

All together: By the Power of Your Word, I am assured that I possess this Gift of Wisdom.

Silent Reflection

Song

Blessed are the peacemakers.

Fruit of the Spirit: Peace

How I cooperate with the Spirit
I must grow in this Gift by spending a definite time in prayer every day, giving Jesus a chance to flood my soul with His Love. I will steep my soul in a profound humility, giving the credit for all the fruit I bear to the living Presence of Christ in my soul. I will accept the hardships of life without being disturbed, seeing God's Love in everything, thereby keeping my inner self in peace, and diffusing this peace to others.

People: Mary, Daughter of the Eternal Father, Mother of the Eternal Son, and Spouse of the Holy Spirit, intercede for us.

Journey into Prayer

Silent Reflection

Teaching and Sharing—and/or spontaneous prayer

Song

FRUITS OF THE SPIRIT

Song

Leader: "What God wants is for you all to be holy." (1 Thess. 4:3)

"Greetings to the Church of God ... to the holy people of Jesus Christ, who are called to take their place among all the saints everywhere, who pray to Our Lord Jesus Christ." (1 Cor. 1:2)

Consideration I

It is important for me to realize that any Christian who remains steady in Faith, rooted in Hope, and persevering in Love is holy. Holiness is not an honor for a privileged few: every Christian is called to holiness: it is the common lot of all the faithful. Holiness begins now because of God's Presence in my soul. I am holy with His holiness.

Silent Reflection

Whoever keeps His Commandments lives in God, and God lives in him. We know that He lives in us by the Spirit that He has given us. (1 John 3:24)

This is the love I mean: not our love for God, but God's Love for us when He sent His Son. (1 John 4:10)

Your body, you know, is the temple of the Holy Spirit, who is in you, since you received Him from God. (1 Cor. 6:19)

Consideration II

Through the merits of Christ, the Father has sent His Spirit to raise me from the condition of a slave to that of an adopted son. Through the exercise of all the Gifts of the Spirit, the degree of my holiness will grow, and I can glorify the Father by clearing the way for Jesus to bear fruit in me.

Silent Reflection

Teaching and Sharing — and/or spontaneous prayer

Examine yourselves to make sure you are in the Faith: test yourselves. Do you acknowledge that Jesus Christ is really in you? If not, you have failed the test. (2 Cor. 13:5-6)

Anybody not living a holy life and not loving his brother is no child of God's. (1 John 3:10)

Now you together are Christ's Body; but each of you is a different part of it. (1 Cor. 12:27)

Be ambitious for the higher gifts. (1 Cor. 12:31)

There is a variety of Gifts but always the same Spirit. There are all sorts of services to be done, but always the same Lord, working in all sorts of different ways in different people; it is the same God who is working in all of these. (1 Cor. 12:4-6)

The Holy Gospel according to St. John 15:9-12; 16-17:

Remain in My Love. If you keep My Commandments, you will remain in My Love, just as I have kept My

Father's Commandments and remain in His Love. I
have told you this so that My own joy may be in you
and your joy be complete. This is My Commandment:
Love one another, as I have loved you.

You did not choose Me; no, I chose you; and I com-
missioned you to go out and to bear fruit, fruit that will
last; and then the Father will give you anything you
ask Him in My Name. What I command you is to love
one another.

At this point, the Liturgy of the Eucharist may be celebrated.

*During the thanksgiving after Communion, the fol-
lowing takes place (or if the Liturgy is not celebrated,
the following continues after Scripture Reading).*

Leader: Each one of us in the praying community bears different kinds of fruit and in different ways:

- Some bear the fruit of Love, Faith, Patience, and Gen-
  tleness, giving Joy to all.
- Some bear the fruit of teaching with Wisdom and
  Knowledge, for the good of all.

- Some bear fruit in suffering patiently and with joy: and these help weak members to have courage.
- Some speak to God in the Spirit to pray for those needs known to God alone.
- Some bear fruit in healing through their talents, their prayer, and their compassion.
- Some bear fruit in prophetic utterances, to give courage and enlighten their brothers.
- Some bear fruit in discernment — able to ascertain true from false prophets — for the good of all.
- Some bear fruit in prayer, building up the Body of Christ.
- Some bear fruit by working unselfishly — for the good of others.
- Some bear fruit by humble obedience to the Church, to parents, and to employers.
- Some bear fruit by caring, and being available to those in need.

*Period of Glorifying the Father by
witnessing to His fruit in our lives.*

Song

Together — Prayer: Our Lady, Spouse of the Holy Spirit, teach me some of your secrets so I may increase in all the Gifts of the Spirit. I wish to express my Faith with humility and love. I desire to forget myself and live only for Jesus, your Son, by being a fruitful member of my praying community and the Church.

Together: St. Michael and all the Holy Angels, make me more aware of the Presence of God within me and around me. Inspire me with good thoughts, and enlighten my mind to see God's Will and accomplish it with love. Protect me, my brothers, from the evil one, and guide me in the path of holiness until I reach the Kingdom.

Song

SHARING GOD TOGETHER

Beginning the Day

"O God, let my words come to Your ears, spare a thought for my sighs. Listen to my cry for help" (Ps. 5:1).

Let my soul rise to You, my God, like the incense of the morning sacrifice. Look upon this day as a holocaust in which I sacrifice my will to You. My weaknesses loom before me and make the brightness of this new day a bleak desert. My past proves I have often failed You, but there is a cry in my heart, a longing in my soul that quiets my thoughts and gives me the courage to tackle this day with renewed vigor.

Does Your Majesty look upon me with compassion as I rise and fall so often? Are You pleased when my desires far exceed my accomplishments? I desire to proclaim Your Goodness from the housetops, but my life barely whispers Your Name. I am a spiritual giant in my goals while the fruit I bear speaks only of little things.

Regardless of my failings, dear God, You have given me a new day in which to begin, a new time to grow, new opportunities to love, new people to care for, new crosses to bear. I dedicate these moments of time You have allotted me to Your Eternal Word living and breathing in His Resurrected Body and present in the Holy Eucharist.

Like Mary, I wish to ponder in my heart the mysteries of this day. I want to see Your Face in the suffering, Your hunger in the poor, Your loneliness in the aged. Let the power of Your Spirit permeate my being so His Presence may radiate through me like a quiet ray of sunshine in a darkened room.

I do not know what new pain, fatigue, suffering, or surprises this day will bring, but I offer it all to You as a drop in the ocean of His suffering and His Redemption.

Let my soul stand tall and strong as the spirit of this world swirls around it. Let my roots go deeper into the soil of Faith that Hope may ever rise higher and higher above the discouragement that so often attacks my being.

For these few passing moments I desire to lose myself in Your Divine Perfections. I raise my mind and heart to You, and as the thought of Your Attributes passes through my being, let something of those perfections cling to my soul like oil on a wound. I do not ask for things beyond me, only that Your Power may penetrate my weakness, Your Compassion break down my cold heart, Your Patience cover my impetuosity, and Your Love mellow my harshness.

"I say this prayer to You, God, for at daybreak You listen for my voice, and at dawn I hold myself in readiness for You." "Let us wake in the morning filled with Your Love and sing and be happy all our days" (Ps. 5:3; 90:14).

Litany of the Divine Attributes

Divine Essence, who alone art holy, I bow before Your Being ...

Response: Let me share Your Holiness.

Divine Unity and Simplicity, in whom there is no complexity ...

Response: Make me simple and sincere.

Divine Eternity, without beginning and without end, giver of immortality ...

Response: Make me good and kind.

Divine Wisdom, who designed the length and depth of creation ...

Response: Make me wise enough to see Your form behind everything.

Divine Power, creating and sustaining all things with an act of Your Will …

Response: Give me strength to accomplish the things You want me to do.

Divine Providence, whose mantle covers every facet of my life with loving care …

Response: Give me perfect trust that I may work for the needs of today without concern for tomorrow.

Divine Knowledge, from whom nothing is hidden and nothing is forgotten …

Response: Let me penetrate the mysteries of Your Being that I may share Your Life.

Divine Immanence, who penetrates all things and stoops to live in me …

Response: Let me radiate Your Son and glorify You through the Holy Spirit.

Divine Infinity, which embraces all possible perfections …

Response: Give me a share in Your perfections so my neighbor may see You in me.

Divine Truth, in whom there is no shadow of
  deception ...
*Response: Make me truthful and honest in my dealings
  with others.*
Divine Light, in whom all things are visible ...
*Response: Enlighten my soul that I may not live in
  darkness.*
Divine Immensity, that fills and contains all things ...
*Response: Possess me through and through that I may be
  all things to all men.*
Divine Mercy, infinite and without measure ...
*Response: Let me forgive and forget with love and
  compassion.*
Divine Peace, ever tranquil and serene in the midst of
  turmoil ...
*Response: Let me maintain a quiet spirit and be strong
  enough to accept adversities with peace.*
Divine Joy, who alone art the source of all
  happiness ...
*Response: Give me that joy that no man can take away
  from me.*

Divine Justice, who judges everything in the light of
truth through the eyes of mercy ...
*Response: Grant I may not judge my neighbor's motives,
but give him the benefit of the doubt.*
Divine Immutability, ever the same and never changing ...
*Response: Make my vacillating will stronger that I may
not stray from the path of holiness.*
Divine Omnipresence, behind me, before me, and
around me ...
*Response: Let me see Your Face in everything so all Your
creation may speak to me of Your beauty.*
Divine Compassion, so patient and understanding ...
*Response: Let me be sympathetic with my neighbor's
needs and give him my love as well as my deeds.*

*Time is allowed here for silent prayer, medita-
tion, or contemplation as the Spirit leads.*

Ending of Morning Prayer

"God, you are my God; I am seeking You, my soul thirsting for You, my flesh longing for You—a land parched, weary and waterless: I long to gaze on You in the Sanctuary and to see Your power and glory.

"Your love is better than life itself, my lips will recite Your praise; all my life I will bless You, in Your Name I lift up my hands; my soul will feast most richly, on my lips a song of joy and in my mouth, praise" (Ps. 63:1-5).

O Mary, my Mother, help me today to be like Jesus in thought, word, and deed.

Midday Renewal

My Jesus, I look back on this morning and find I have had some success and some failure in my efforts to be like You. There were times my cross seemed unbearable and other times I did not know it was there.

There were people in my path who touched off painful weaknesses in my soul—weaknesses I did not want to see. I forgot Your many disguises and failed to appreciate the opportunity to change and be more like You. I humbly acknowledge my faults and put them all in the furnace of Your Love. Consume them, refine them like tarnished gold in the fire, and let the purifying power of Your Spirit renew my soul for greater things this afternoon.

Give to those I have offended many graces; make them holy. Bless those who have offended me and forgive them, for they did not mean to hurt me.

Give courage to the sick whose nerves are frayed from pain and whose strength is almost gone. Snatch sinners from destruction and give them the grace of final repentance.

I place at Your feet the sins of the world ...

Response: Precious Blood of Jesus, wipe them away.

I place in Your Heart the coldness of Your
　　creatures ...

Response: Sacred Heart of Jesus, inflame them with love.

I place in Your Mercy prisoners, dope addicts, alcoholics, the bored, and those in despair ...

*Response: Merciful Jesus, touch their souls with the living
　　water of Grace.*

I place in Your Arms the aged, the youth, the retarded, the working man and his family ...

Response: Provident Jesus, keep them all in Your care.

There may be time here for personal intentions.

Lord Jesus, give me an awareness of Your Divine Presence within me and my neighbor. Let the radiance of that Presence shine ever brighter in my soul despite the frailties within it.

Let me rise after every fall with renewed hope in Your powerful grace and let my love reach the most abandoned. I place this afternoon in Your Hands so it may rise to the Father as a pleasing sacrifice.

I thank You, O God, with all my heart, because You have heard what I have said. In the presence of the Angels I play for you and bow down towards Your holy Temple.

I give thanks to Your Name for Your Love and faithfulness; Your promise is even greater than Your fame. The day I called for help You heard me and You increased my strength.

Though I live surrounded by trouble, You keep me alive. You stretch Your hand out and save me; Your right hand will do everything for me. (Ps. 138:1-3; 7, 8)

End of the Day

The day is over, my Lord. I thank You for it all. I wish I had corresponded to the Sacrament of the Moment in a more fervent way, but I give you instead a humbled heart.

I did acquire self-knowledge and that is the beginning of wisdom. Your grace was ever present though I did not always use its power. It has been a good day, for my failings have given me self-knowledge and my successes have manifested Your Presence in me. This has been Your work, Holy Spirit, and I praise You for it. You use every scrap of my weaknesses to make me humble, every virtue to make me more like Jesus, every opportunity to increase grace in my soul, every circumstance to show me His Will. You are the Sanctifier, the Spirit sent to heal my wounds and give me a new birth.

I rest tonight secure because Your Love for me is beyond my unworthiness and surpasses all understanding. I unite my love to the love of Jesus and offer it to You in reparation for all the coldness and indifference in the world. My day proved to me that I do not love You as I ought. My will is strong, and I cling to it and find it hard to unite it to Your Will. And yet, this is the proof of love. It is not my knowledge of Your Goodness, or the consolations of Your Presence that draws You to my soul—no, it is my need for Your Mercy. My emptiness calls out for Your Love, and my nothingness reaches for Your creative Power to change me, mold me, and sanctify me.

There were times today when my soul was trapped between the world and my own selfishness—a time when darkness enveloped me as if to swallow me up in the tomb of hopelessness. Was it not Your Presence that seemed to clasp my hand and guide my faltering steps to a new dawn? Was I not somehow made cleaner by the passage through darkness and desperation? Your ways are truly not my ways, but they are more certain than the sun that rises in the morning.

A short meditation may be made here.

Ending Prayer

The battles of today are over, and I come home wounded but determined to attain greater heights tomorrow. Your Grace in me is more powerful than my weaknesses.

I give You my sleep tonight and I ask that as my body rests, my heart and soul may rest in Your Love. Let Faith quiet the fear that torments me in the night. Let Hope relax my conscience with trust in Your Mercy. Let Love surround me like a blanket so the silence of the night may be like Your gentle voice singing me to sleep.

Instill within me that confidence that knows "no disaster can overtake me for You have put Your Angels in charge of me to guard me wherever I go. You rescue all who cling to You. You protect me because I know Your Name. You answer me whenever I invoke You and You are with me when I am in trouble" (Ps. 91:10-11, 14-15).

Protect me from the Enemy as I lay down my defenses to prepare for new battles tomorrow. Let my thoughts be in Your Heaven as my body rests in exile. Listen to the pleas of Mary as she intercedes in my behalf. Do not remember my sins, but rather clothe me with the cloak of innocence.

Good Night, dear God, and may every breath I take this night praise Your Holy Name.

RAMBLING THOUGHTS

The present moment resembles a sacrament—resembles many sacraments. It gives me Jesus like the Eucharist; it gives me the opportunity to forgive and be forgiven like Confession; it enhances His Presence in my soul like Baptism; it puts in operation the seven gifts like Confirmation. His Spirit gives me power to be transformed into Jesus like the Mass and affords me opportunities to die to self and be healed of my faults.

As the priest raises up the Bread and Wine and says, "This is my body," the Spirit of God says, "So be it." Is the Present Moment not like this bread? In it seems nothing worthwhile—nothing attractive—nothing powerful, but if I raise it up to God—if I encounter Him within the mystery of its shadows—its plainness—its monotony—its pain—if I offer the bread of my life, my personality, my heart, my entire self and embrace that moment with love, with Jesus, will He not say, "This is my body"? Will His Spirit not say, "Amen"? Can this embodiment of faults and weaknesses become so holy—so like Jesus, that the Father will one day look at this soul and say, "This is my son—this is my image?"

Will the power of His Spirit absorb my nothingness and sins —change them—transform them? Yes, His Blood merited this gift, this privilege, this transformation, this miracle of grace, this "greater work."

If only I could live in the Will of God—in His Spirit—in His Love. If I could only see His Providence, His Spirit at work in the present moment. He works, arranges, permits every facet of my life, every moment of my existence. His Presence is in the midst of my everyday situations. The only Reality is within the reality of whatever is happening. If only I could embrace the present moment as if He were in front of me. The present moment is like a chisel in the hands of God. He uses it to round off jagged corners, smooth over rough surfaces, reshape and remold my soul. It is precious, for it brings God to me in a personal way. It calls forth the very best of the One who lives within me. My God, let me embrace the present moment with love.

My Jesus, my poor soul is surrounded by distress and frustration. You seem so far away, and though my faith tells me you are near, my soul cries out to see Your Face. I desire to live by faith because I know you are pleased as a soul hangs on when all seems lost. Do you mind if I wish You were by my side so I could reach out and touch you? Do I see You shake Your head in wonderment at my lack of perception? Yes, I know — I do touch You when my neighbor needs me — it is You who smile when I pass a child — it is You who give me strength to go another mile — another day. Your Presence surrounds me like a gentle breeze. Your Spirit tugs at my heart to spur me on. Your Father calls me His child. I desire what I already possess — I look for Someone who is so close I cannot see Him. I look for a staff that is already in my hand.

Your Will, my God, is beyond my comprehension. I so often rebel and cry out to You as if You did not hear. My soul looks for You, and my rebellion builds up an invisible wall between us. My pride makes me think you have not heard my plea, or your justice has shut me off from seeing your Face. My poor soul is in turmoil at the thought of losing You. I am torn between the pride that rebels and the need that cries out for help. One part of me says that what is happening is unfair, unjust, cold, and cruel, and yet deep in the recesses of my soul there is that faint voice that assures me Your Will is holy, just, and infinitely wise. My rebellion and my desire to do Your Will totally vie with each other for the possession of my soul. I am numb with the struggle. My soul is parched and weary. I stand before Your holy, silent Presence, clinging to my desire to love You alone with all my heart—hoping You will not hear the turmoil nor see my misery. All the while I know it is this very wretched state that attracts Your Mercy and I cling to the anchor that is inscribed with the words, "My power is at its best in weakness" (2 Cor. 12:9).

Your Presence surrounds me like a cloak. It penetrates my being like the warm rays of the sun. When I remain in You, as You remain in me, no trial is too difficult, no pain unendurable.

Then suddenly, it is as if darkness envelops my soul and I am forced to stand still, waiting and reaching out to touch You. My steps falter and hesitate — my heart fails in courage — my eyes see no distinguishing form — my ears strain for the slightest sound of Your Voice — I wait as a helpless child — I wait for the dawn.

My mind questions and my heart ponders Your ways. Your Wisdom permits trials in my life that I cannot understand. I look around in wonderment, seeking an answer — a possible solution. When I pray, You seem far away, almost not hearing me. I feel an emptiness in my soul as if this trial has drained my strength — my being stands before You rather than petitions for help. I stand waiting, empty, silent before Holiness Itself — not understanding — afraid to express my thoughts, but knowing Your Love penetrates my soul and hears my silent groanings. My head is bowed down as I struggle to penetrate Your Ways. Then it is, in the silence of Your Presence, that I see the reason for it all. My soul before Baptism was like fine tissue paper — fragile, weak, unable to withstand even a breeze. Then Your Spirit was given to me at Baptism and Living Water began to saturate that tissue paper. The special Water enables my tissue paper to stand before You and live. Without that Water, that covering, it would dissolve before the fire of Your Presence—so holy, so powerful. I see now—it is so clear. Trials and sufferings—my moment to moment choices, pour more and more of that Living Water into my tissue paper—my being. Not only am I able to stand before You covered with this strength, but I am able to get closer and closer to that Fire. I may even one day be in the center of that Flame. The opportunity to be one with You is mine by the power of Your Spirit and the Blood of Jesus. I have only to trust Your Wisdom, accomplish Your Will, and love with Your Love. The trials You send me, the dryness in my soul, provide more and more Living Water to saturate my soul so it may one day look at You, my Lord and God and say, "Abba, Father."

My life is like a jar filled with sand. Some of the sand is clean, some darkened by the wind of sufferings, some has become chunky and hard from disappointments. The Father looks down on me with compassion. He doesn't take out large scoops of sand at one time. He knows it would be more than I could endure. He permits me to cooperate with Him so the sand and debris slowly disappear and I hardly feel the loss. He begins by pouring Living Water into my jar—He adds before He takes away. That Water stirs up my soul—I begin to see the dirty sand, the debris and garbage. Then suddenly it settles, and there is less sand and more clean water. Time passes and something happens—a decision to make, an opportunity to be like Jesus. Once again it settles with more Water and less sand. I begin to realize the value of self-knowledge, of trials and sufferings. My heart desires more of that Living Water, my little jar begins to expand and contract in its effort to obtain more of God. Suddenly, little cracks appear, tiny holes through which the sand begins to flow freely. Dryness of soul increases my thirst for the Living Water. Then begins the process of losing and gaining, of dying and living, of thirsting and being filled. I begin to seek opportunities to be like Jesus. I poke holes in my jar so more sand can leave and more of Him fill my jar. Slowly, sometimes painfully, I make right decisions—I choose Him over myself—I choose His Will over mine—I love when it is hard to love—believe when all is darkness—hope when all seems lost. A beautiful process begins. The Living Water overflows and passes through all the little holes in my jar. It slakes the thirst of my neighbor, who doesn't know his jar too is full of sand—he too needs Living Water. I can trust my day, my life to God—He does know best—His Wisdom is beyond my understanding.

Where are You, O God? My soul cries out to You, and I hear my voice resound like an echo in a deep cavern. All around me is darkness and I cannot see Your Face or hear Your Voice. There is no star in the night, no glimmer of light. I walk on, one step at a time, hoping my hand will somehow brush against Yours and I will know all is well. Each step brings new anguish and new disappointments. I would not mind the darkness if I knew You were there, but then would it be darkness? Would not that realization be like a sudden burst of sunshine? Faith tells me You live in me—a hidden Presence in the depths of my soul—a Presence in the darkness of my anguish—a Presence guiding my steps—a Power in my weakness—Light hiding Itself until I grow strong enough to live in Light forever—truly. Truly, we walk together until one day Light will draw light from the darkness.

My constant companion today is pain — throbbing, gnawing, constant pain. Its presence seems to push out every thought of You, my Jesus. Your Presence vies with suffering for my attention. The two are not compatible at this moment. And yet, is it so? Is it pain or self-pity that distracts me from You? Pain is a strong feeling, and Your Presence is a faith experience — dry, searching. If You gave me great consolation with my pain, one good feeling would have to overpower a painful feeling. That would be a kind of spiritual pain reliever. Like aspirin, it would last a short time and once more the battle for dominance would rage. Is there a light You wish to give me, my Lord? Is there a point I am missing? Have I not missed the forest for the trees? Yes, instead of seeing us together, my Jesus, I have seen us apart — You, way up there somewhere and poor me down here looking up for help and relief. What I have failed to realize is that You have already given me relief through medicine and doctors and the pain that remains is also You — really You. You are not only *in* the pain — You suffer that pain with me. You do not permit suffering in my life and then stand back and observe my reaction. No, You suffer every throb with me, for You told us that when we are sick and someone visits us, comforts us, eases our discomfort, they are giving that loving care to You! I do not need to seek You outside my suffering. I do not need to explain each pain. You feel it with me—we are united—my pain is Yours, and Your pain is mine. I am healed as I feel each throb; I am transformed as I accept each new opportunity; I am more powerful as I am more aware of my weakness. My eyes slowly turn towards Yours, and we catch each other's tears in the cup of the Father's Will. The Love in Your Heart touches mine, and new strength surges through me as together we give ourselves—for the salvation of souls. "I make up in my body what is wanting in the sufferings of Christ" (Col. 1:24). Your Presence is so close I do not see it—Your pain so entwined with mine, I do not distinguish it from my feelings. You are so close I almost miss You completely. No wonder, I seek and do not find. How can one seek one who is not missing, look for one already present, cry out to one who knows his very thoughts? Yes, my pain is only half a share—a small portion. You bear it too. It suddenly seems so little.

My Lord, show me Your Will. My faith wavers at times because Your Providence in my life unfolds itself only in minute ways. Like the pieces of a giant mosaic, I see only a small piece at a time. I cannot see or understand the place of each piece or how it adds to the beauty of the whole. Every piece, by itself, appears so insignificant and its beauty of little account. I must trust that this cross, pain, misunderstanding, and humiliation are all part of the mosaic that portrays my life and its ascent to You. I place myself and those I may have unconsciously offended in Your Heart. I ask that You comfort them and enlighten them. Give them peace and understanding, and let Your will be done in their lives as well as mine.

Lord, Father, give me the grace to understand how my soul is made to Your image. A Voice spoke a Word, and the power of that Voice in the Word created the universe. You, Lord Father, are the Voice; the Word You forever speak is Jesus, and the power is the Spirit. Let my thoughts be expressed by Your Word, and let the power of Your Spirit touch all hearts that hear that Word. Human words merely convey knowledge or messages, but when my thoughts are compassionate and merciful, the words that express those thoughts are humble and kind. There is great power in these fruits of the Spirit. Let me step aside and permit Him to express Jesus through me in the present moment. Let Your Trinitarian life be manifest in my soul by my love for my neighbor and my union with Your Will.

The trials and anxieties of daily life are like a cloud that makes my walk with You hard and uncertain. My horizon seems only as far as my own footprints. Questions and doubts swirl around my thoughts and make clear decisions difficult. Then it is I realize that somehow I have permitted myself, people and things to so possess my thoughts that all is a maze of confusion. I have looked "down" and "at" instead of "up" and "to" You. My soul is brought to order only by the remembrance of Your awesome, silent Presence — a Presence that brings to light the pettiness of things that disturb me. The deep reality of Your Presence in the present moment and in my soul dispels my anxieties and doubts. Grant that I may ever keep my eyes on You and find my hope in the accomplishment of Your Holy Will.

O God, Your power is so manifest in a storm and Your beauty in a sunrise, and yet I do not see Your Power at work in the storms of my life or Your Goodness in the joys that follow. It seems it is always easier to see Your hand in the lives of others, or in nature. My faith is weak, Lord; increase my faith. Let Your Divine Presence in the events of the present moment be as visible to me as the storm or sunrise. Let Your Wisdom come to mind when I do not understand the reasoning or lack of reasoning in the trials of life. Injustice leads to resentment, persecution leads to anger; lack of compassion for myself leads to guilt—all these things buffet my soul when I lose sight of You, O God. Lead me by the hand, guide my steps, inspire my heart to see You in all things.

LOVE AND SALVATION

No Greater Love

Proven Love

There is a need in every human being to love and to be loved. There is also a need to manifest that love. Unfortunately, each person's concept of proving love is so varied that the recipient often misses the proof.

One person's idea of proving love is by doing things — buying gifts and being thoughtful. A husband may prove love by being a good provider, and a wife by being a good cook.

Children prove love by being obedient, and an absence of obedience brings true love into question. Friends manifest love by companionship and mutual goals.

All these manifestations of love entail something nice — something pleasant — something good. However, the way love is proven to us may not be to our liking, and we often refuse to accept the particular way one individual proves his love.

We miss important signs of love because we refuse, consciously or unconsciously, to accept the way others prove their love for us.

Lack of acceptance of the particular and sometimes peculiar way others manifest their love causes agony and loneliness in the human heart. We are constantly being offended by what we think is a lack of attention on the part of those we love.

Misunderstanding causes coldness and dissension because the human heart, desiring so much to be loved, is not willing to accept the way one person expresses love.

We are often demanding in our desire for love, and little signs of affection from friends and family are missed in a maze of selfishness.

Parents sometimes demand an "all A" scholastic average from their children as a proof of love. Though love is never mentioned, the disappointment over the laborious acquisition of an "F" puts the emphasis on a wrong set of values. Effort is not appreciated as a mark of love; a high grade is demanded instead.

Even gifts are accepted with a visible lack of appreciation because that particular item was not our idea of a gift — of a manifestation of love.

Life becomes very complicated when we wait for others to manifest love in the way we desire. Our temperaments, personalities, tastes, likes, and dislikes are so different that it is impossible to always manifest love to the satisfaction of everyone.

Perhaps this is the reason Jesus asked us to love as He loves. It is part of loving unselfishly when we accept and are attuned to the least manifestation of love from others and appreciate their particular signs of affection.

As we miss signs of love from our neighbor, we also miss them from God. God is constantly doing loving things for each one of us. He is always providing, protecting, nourishing, forgiving, and loving us. Not a moment of our life passes that He has not done something good to us or for us.

Why do so many of us go through life with never an act of praise or thanksgiving to God for all His consistent, loving attention?

One reason people miss this loving attention is because they treat God in the same way they treat their neighbor. God's way of manifesting His love for them is never the way they think it should be.

We seldom thank Him for our birth but often question His purpose in creating us. We seldom thank Him for health, talent, or strength, but He is the first to hear our complaints if we lose any of these qualities.

We take our breath, sight, and hearing for granted and are only aware of the awesome wonder of these faculties when they are gone or gradually slip away from us. Then we look to God as an unjust Creator who took something from us that was rightfully ours.

We are, on the whole, an assorted lot of odd people who cry out to God in anguish of heart when we are in need and expect an immediate reply as a proof of His love and concern. We never question our wisdom, but we analyze and tear apart His judgments in our regard.

If we are to see God's signs of love in our individual lives and not run the risk of living in darkness, we must look at the life of Jesus and see what proofs of love He gave to each one of us.

The signs of love He gave may not be to our liking but that is our fault, not His. If we become attuned to God's constant proof of love for us, then we shall become more attuned to the many signs of affection others try to give us.

Silent Love

Isaiah had prophesied that when the world was in quiet silence — in the dead of night — the Eternal Son would leap down and dwell among us (Wisd. 18:14-15). It is so strange that the Father chose such a quiet time.

Men and women had waited and prayed for this great occasion, and yet it happened as if it were to be a great secret — a secret the angels and the stars could not keep. Spiritual beings with great intelligences revealed the secret to uneducated shepherds. An inanimate star revealed the secret to Wise Men, men of high human intelligence.

God's love for us seems to take delight in contradictions. It is as if He desired us to seek Him out. The greatest marvel of all is that He came and lived as one of us.

Is there any human being who could ever understand the humiliation of a God becoming man? Our pride is so great that this sign of love on the part of God is lost to most of us.

It is something like a genius becoming an ant just because he loved ants! This simile is as nothing compared to God becoming man, because both the genius and the ant are created beings.

When we think of the Uncreated lowering Himself to the level of His creatures, we get some small idea as to why the angels and stars had to proclaim this unprecedented act of love.

Unfortunately, most men were asleep for this momentous occasion and missed the whisper of God in the cry of a Child saying, "I love you."

Most men, running after their toys and playthings, do not hear the Silent Love of God in the life of Jesus.

Perhaps this is true because we do not equate proving love with sacrifice or pain, and yet as we contemplate the life of Jesus we find that almost every act of love, both for His Father and us, was sacrificial or painful.

Is this why fewer marriages are successful, fewer friendships lasting, fewer heroes admired and why fewer men and women have the determination to become holy as He is holy? We are becoming more selfish in our attitudes and with that selfishness, that lack of desire to sacrifice for our neighbor, comes a loneliness that has never been experienced before by so many people all over the world.

The days of chivalry need not be over. The days when rich men become poor and poor men lose home and land for God, need not be a thing of the past or a hope of the future: it can be now.

There must be in every Christian that silent witness of love, that strength of character that comes from a voluntary sacrifice made out of love.

St. Paul put it beautifully when he told the Philippians. "His state was Divine yet He did not cling to His equality with God but emptied Himself to assume the condition of a slave" (Phil. 2:6-7).

How many of us practice this Silent Love for our neighbor? We find it so difficult to give up our opinions, our will, and our desires when the good of the whole is at stake. We cannot empty our hearts of the desire to be right, to be considered talented, to be successful in every undertaking.

Are we willing to see others, younger and brighter, do the things we wanted to do and couldn't? Because Silent Love is not a part of our daily lives, the young are impatient with the old, the aged are envious of the young, the middle-aged think the whole world is in their hands with no thought of tomorrow, and many regret their yesterdays. They do not want to step aside or to rejoice at the talents others possess — others who are younger or older.

Love does away with discontent, disquietude, and discouragement. It willingly steps aside. It is willing to drop an argument when nothing good is to be accomplished—willing to be considered wrong though God knows it is right.

Silent Love prefers others to itself as Jesus did. It is willing to accept a lesser portion, provided the one it loves has a greater portion. It is willing to leave all things, including itself, for the sake of the Kingdom and the good of its neighbor.

As we think of the witness of Silent Love, we realize that Jesus preferred this kind of love even after His appearance on earth. He was born in a stable—with cold and wind—with only the Silent Love of Mary, Joseph, and the shepherds. The thought of any noise at this awesome time makes the soul recoil. The whole event was one of Silent Love. He was content that only those in future centuries would appreciate this solemn moment. He endured the indifference of the world because His Love rose above tepidity.

He would silently love men from afar—from a cold cave. His love stood strong like a sentinel in the night—watching over those who were totally unaware of His Presence.

Are we ever content to love from afar? We all find Silent Love difficult to give and even more difficult to receive. We want love to show and yet, who can say He did not love us by enduring the world's indifference — by lovingly accomplishing the Father's Will?

He was born in the midst of men's lukewarmness and died in the midst of their opprobrium. His love may have been Silent to many of His time, and they may have complained that He should have come in a flare of celestial glory and forced Himself upon them. But part of God's Love was Silent and He was content to be in their midst silently loving them and caring for them without recompense, without return.

In the life of every human being there are those we must love from afar. There are those who hate us, are annoyed by our presence and irked by our opinions. Our love for them must be constant though it is silent. We must "love our enemies and pray for those who persecute us" (Matt. 5:43-48). This is certainly Silent Love, for an enemy is not aware of our love — his hatred blinds his discernment of love.

There are many ways we can and should practice Silent Love. The old must love those who have forgotten them. The young must love their parents with that strong love that is often silent because vocation or circumstances make outward signs of love impossible.

There must be in the heart of every Christian a Silent Love for all the unknown people in the world—people of other faiths, other nations, other cultures. There must be that Silent Love for Country—the kind that is not afraid to see its weaknesses, but strong enough to defend its principles if the need arises.

There is the Silent Love we have for all the sick and downtrodden, the starving and homeless all over the world. Without this Silent Love ever burning in our hearts we will become indifferent when others are in need. Their plight and pain will never touch our hearts for our hearts will be steeped in selfishness if they are not filled with Silent Love—a love that is always ready to be tapped—always ready to reach out and touch those in need as soon as a need is apparent.

Hidden Love

The love some people manifest is very hidden, and this is as God wills. When a friend defends the reputation of a neighbor who is being maligned, that friend is manifesting a Hidden Love. The person criticized may never know of this act of loyalty, but God will reward it because it is most like His own Love.

Jesus counseled His Apostles very often to practice this kind of love. One day He said to them, "Be careful not to parade your good deeds before men to attract their notice. When you give alms, do not have it trumpeted before you.... Your left hand must not know what your right is doing: your almsgiving must be secret, and your Father who sees all that is done in secret will reward you" (Matt. 6:1-4).

The accomplishment of many good deeds must be accompanied by Hidden Love, for Paul reminds us that if we gave all our possessions to the poor without love it would be nothing (1 Cor. 13:2). But Jesus wants both the love and the deed to be hidden. If we do not know the cause or person responsible for some act of charity done for us, then we cannot return that act of love. That particular act of kindness is hidden as is the love behind it.

God wants our love to be hidden in some instances, to purify our motives. Jesus told His Apostles that when we do an act of kindness that is known only to the Father, the Father returns that deed — that act of love — with a reward.

This kind of hidden love — hidden from our neighbor — is the kind that is most like God's Love. Because a hidden act of love resembles God's pure love for us, we become, by that act, more like Him.

Hidden Love is the kind that expects no return because great care is taken that the recipient is unaware of it. Hidden Love takes such pleasure in seeing the recipient benefited in any way, that personal recognition is out of the question.

There are many ways the average person practices hidden love, and most of the recipients of that love are never aware of their benefactors.

A man may work extra hours to provide some comfort for his family, but the family may completely lose sight of the extra love manifested. A wife may spend much time over a hot stove preparing extra food for some feast day, and the family be totally unaware that she may not have felt well at the time.

A smile on the face of one in pain contains a hidden power whose true source is known only to God. How many people keep great trials away from loved ones in order not to burden them with more pain?

Jesus wanted us to love our neighbor with a pure love, and although it is not possible for all our love to be hidden, there are times when a manifestation of love brings only more attention to ourselves.

Jesus asked us to bear fruit for all men to see, but the fruit must not be borne for the motive of self-glory. "When you pray," He told His followers, "do not imitate the hypocrites: they love to say their prayers standing in the synagogues and at street corners for people to see them" (Matt. 6:5). Here we see the motive for a good deed was the glorification of self and the praise of men. An occasion was created in which the reward would immediately follow the deed.

Hidden Love, on the contrary, is humble and willing to be overlooked here, to patiently wait for the reward hereafter. "When you pray," Jesus advised the crowd, "go to your private room ... pray to your Father who is in that secret place, and your Father who sees all that is done in secret will reward you" (Matt. 6:6).

Hidden Love extends to our spiritual lives. Though it is good to share our thoughts and graces with our neighbor, it is necessary to keep our interior a hidden sanctuary where only God lives, reigns, and to which He alone has access. Our prayers, as we witness by Sunday Worship, edify our neighbor by a communal witness, but our prayers must rise to Heaven every day as an incense of praise and petition for all the temporal and spiritual needs of our neighbor—and this is done in secret.

Being gentle during a tense situation can hide a painful interior struggle for self-control. No one knows how hard it is for us to control our temper. This is because we don't often equate virtue with love. We all know that love must motivate us, but we seldom consider virtue in itself a manifestation of personal love.

St. Paul realized this aspect of love when he told the Corinthians that love was kind, patient, and long suffering. An act of kindness is in itself a manifestation of love. It is not only the fruit of love — it is love itself.

Do we realize that when our neighbor is kind to us he is saying, "I love you"? Do we understand the love behind a patient answer to a critical statement? There are those who do not know how to love or find it difficult to say, "I love you"; but they do possess the ability to show love by being kind and patient friends.

Love has a hidden quality — a spirit of caring that is never selfish. Though St. Paul tells us that love is always patient and kind, he also explained what love is not.

"Love," Paul said, "is never jealous" (1 Cor. 13:4); so when we wish someone success, we are saying, "I love you." "Love is never boastful or conceited" (1 Cor. 13:4-5); so when we

242

listen to others and do not make ourselves seem better than they, we are saying, "I love you." "Love is never rude or selfish"; and so when we are polite and generous with our time and our talents, we are saying, "I love you."

Perhaps one of the most hidden qualities of love is that it does not "take offense or feel resentful" (1 Cor. 13:5). When we are oversensitive to what people say, or how they look at us, or what they think of us, we are not loving them. When we resent their contrary opinions and personality traits, we are not loving them. It is when we are tolerant, understanding, and objective with our neighbor that we are saying we love him. Our neighbor may never see our love when we are patient or kind to him, but before God we have loved rather than hated and been gentle rather than angry. This is why St. Paul said that "love never comes to an end" (1 Cor. 13:8). It is a lasting quality of soul — independent of every exterior influence: it is hidden in its essence and merely shows a small part of its beauty exteriorly.

Love does not desire its own satisfaction — it desires only to please the one on whom it spends itself. Love is sincere, humble, selfless, and ready for any sacrifice. It must render some service to every human being with whom it lives or works. The

Hidden quality of love manifests itself in the way we behave towards our neighbor. Though most people do not think of us as being loving when we are patient, they are very much aware of how unloving we are when we are impatient.

This Hidden Love holds families together and when it is missing, there is in the family a veritable hell. Selfishness destroys people and nations because the Hidden quality of love is missing. When no one in a family renders any hidden services for the others, that family becomes more and more distant—a house becomes a motel with brothers and sisters as residents.

There must be a spirit of love between ourselves and our fellow men—a spirit that brings peace wherever we go and gives joy to all those we meet.

We are not always in a position to give food or alleviate pain, but we can always give love and then, who knows, those in pain may suddenly feel all is well.

Corrective Love

"Jerusalem, Jerusalem, you that kill the Prophets and stone those who are sent to you! How often have I longed to gather your children as a hen gathers her chicks under her wings, and you refused" (Matt. 23:37).

One of the most difficult aspects of love is its corrective quality. We see Jesus weeping over a people He loved who did not love Him in return. His complaints against this people were not always hidden as the above quotation indicates. He lashed out at the lawyers, Scribes, and Pharisees for their hypocrisy, but cloaked in those angry words was a heart full of love.

Jesus tried to bring out their hidden faults, their secret motives and their hypocritical actions, but they did not accept this aspect of God's love: they did not fathom the depths of His love.

Jesus knew that every time He corrected anyone, even the Apostles, He ran the risk of losing their friendship, but His love was totally unselfish. He sought the love of others not for His sake but for theirs.

His love was pure: it sought only the good of the one He loved and never sought any advantage for Himself. This is why He could correct His Apostles when they fell short of His expectations.

When Peter made his profession of faith in the Divinity of Christ, Jesus called Him "Rock" and promised to build His

Church on that rock. But when Peter's human nature took over and he rebelled against the thought of Jesus' death, Jesus called him "Satan" (Matt. 16:18, 23). In the Upper Room at the Last Supper, Peter would not permit Jesus to wash his feet and Jesus reminded him that unless he accepted the humility of the Gospel and lived by it, he would be separated from his Master forever (John 13:8). Jesus did not hesitate to correct Peter, but His motive for doing so was His love for Peter.

It is difficult to correct anyone, but love makes it possible and gentle Love takes out the sting of correction so the person being rebuked understands that loving concern is behind the reprimand.

When selfish anger is mixed with a correction, the tone of voice and lack of reason makes the correction difficult to accept.

Pride rebels against correction but love makes correction possible and bearable. Because God is our father, He prunes us and shows us our weaknesses. The self-knowledge that makes us so miserable at times is a special light from our Father, who sees us and knows us perfectly.

His Wisdom arranges and rearranges every facet of our lives in order to make us aware of those areas that need change.

It is His special sign of love. Though it is difficult to see His love in all our trials and pains, we can at least recognize His work by looking into our past and realizing how He works in our daily lives.

St. Paul told the Hebrews that God was treating them as sons when He corrected them. We see this quiet love in Jesus when He knew His Apostles were stooping to petty ambitions. "What were you arguing about on the road?" Jesus asked them. The Apostles were embarrassed and said nothing in reply (Mark 9:3). Their silence did not prevent Jesus from taking the opportunity to expose and heal their ambitious desires.

So He sat down, called the Twelve to Him and said, "If anyone wants to be first, he must make himself last of all and servant of all" (Mark 9:35). Jesus did not object to their desire to be great in the Kingdom, but when their ambitions became worldly, proud, and arrogant, He was compelled by love to show them true greatness. They desired to be first for their own sakes — to have the pleasure of lording over others — but Jesus made them understand true greatness.

In the kingdom of this world, men seek to be first. In the Kingdom of God, men must seek to be last and God Himself will raise them up. Lest they misunderstand His reprimand and exaggerate His demands, "He took a little child, set him in front of them, put His arms around him, and said to them, 'Anyone who welcomes one of these little children in My Name, welcomes Me; and anyone who welcomes Me, welcomes not Me but the One who sent Me'" (Mark 9:37).

His love for them did not blind Him to their faults, and it did not prevent Him from correcting dangerous weaknesses. The Apostles were beginning to think more of themselves and their individual positions in the Kingdom than the Kingdom itself. Self-gratification was uppermost in their minds. Suddenly, their lives became complicated. Their initial enthusiasm to follow Jesus and be with Him degenerated into a desire for personal glory.

When they first began to follow Him, they were like children; their only thought was of Jesus and their zeal to preach the Good News drove them to make many sacrifices. But when the powers Jesus gave them caused them to be sought out by the people, their minds began to turn inward and they lost that simplicity so necessary to do great things. They began to argue among themselves and entertain thoughts of jealousy.

Any other leader might not have corrected them as Jesus did. A leader of today might find such a scene interesting and look upon the survivor of such intrigue as a strong man while those who lost were weak.

Jesus saw the good in each Apostle. He told them all that true greatness consisted in being a servant of all and not in being served by all. His love made His correction gentle and instructive. He not only told them they were wrong but explained what they should do to be pleasing to the Father.

Corrective Love not only sees failures but explains why those weaknesses are wrong and what can be done to change them.

We see, however, that the love of Jesus was not always gentle in correcting. There are souls whose state of sin is so deep, only a severe correction can penetrate through the layers of rationalization that make one a hardened sinner.

In St. John's Gospel we read that "just before the Jewish Passover Jesus went up to Jerusalem and in the Temple He found people selling cattle, sheep and pigeons, and the money-changers sitting at their counters there. Making a whip out of some cords, He drove them all out of the Temple, cattle and sheep as well, scattered the money-changers' coins, knocked their tables over and said to the pigeon-sellers, 'Take all this out of here and stop turning my Father's house into a market'" (John 2:13-17).

The Corrective Love of Jesus was enhanced or tempered according to the need of the person being corrected. In this incident we find Jesus driving out the sheep and cattle with a rope. We see His anger blaze as He upsets money tables and the coins of various nations splatter all over the courtyard. The money-changers seemed to be the main object of His wrath. He looked angrily at those money-changers and said, "My house shall be called a house of prayer for all the people but you have turned it into a robbers' den" (Mark 11:17-18).

The business outside the Temple was a legitimate business. People from all nations had to buy cattle and sheep to sacrifice and exchange their money for the coin of the realm. The poor who did not have money or cattle to offer for the presentation of their firstborn sons bought pigeons.

But what began as a necessity turned into evil, and greedy men used the innocence of foreigners to cheat and steal and did this in the Temple precincts! The anger of Jesus was just, and because it was not self-centered He had the presence of mind to regulate His anger. When He saw those who sold the pigeons to the poor, He merely asked them to take their pigeons and remove them from the Temple.

The beautiful courtyard of His Father's House had become the scene of lying and cheating and was full of the noise of a marketplace. The peace and beauty that was once there, designed to prepare the heart for prayer, was gone. His zeal was fanned into anger—a just anger—an anger that was concerned for His Father's glory. There is one aspect of this account that often escapes the eye. The whipping and the overturning of tables was an outward manifestation of the degree of evil these people had fallen into.

It was a reprimand brought about by the Corrective Love in the Heart of Jesus. All the world would know from that day forward exactly how God felt about mixing greed and the spirit of this world with worship. All those who were the victims of His anger could, if they so willed, learn a lesson, repent of their sins and help make God's Temple the House of Prayer He meant it to be.

There are many other incidents of the Corrective Love of Jesus in the Gospels, but we can see by the few mentioned that a sincere, deep love cannot stand by while those it loves destroy themselves. It may happen that after reprimands, warnings, and corrections, those we love do not change, but there our Corrective Love manifests itself in prayer. It petitions and pleads with the Father to enlighten and forgive all those whose will is turned against Him.

Corrective Love is ever vigilant, watchful, and gentle. It is unselfish and unafraid. It is often misunderstood and more often misinterpreted, but it perseveres to the end, ever loving and ever caring.

Patient Love

There is in each of us an element of love that is willing to wait. This is one of the consoling qualities of God's Love for us. The Father's Love does not diminish when we offend Him: it is our love that has diminished. We have at some given moment loved ourselves more than God. We have also preferred ourselves over God, and the result of such an action is sin.

When our neighbor in turn offends us, we are very unlike God, for our love for that neighbor lessens. It is similar to our electric lights dimming during a storm—one phase of the electrical system momentarily turns off and every bulb loses power.

Though the one who offends us or insults us has less love for us at that moment, our own love for him must continue.

We must be patient with the weaknesses of our neighbor and be willing to wait with love, for some manifest change in his life.

One day Peter asked Jesus how many times he should forgive his neighbor. In other words, how long should he wait for his neighbor to overcome his weaknesses. Peter thought that if he forgave his brother seven times it would certainly be long enough in time and generous enough in mercy. Jesus' reply was "Not seven, I tell you, but seventy-seven times" (Matt. 18:21-22).

We may not be conscious of loving when we forgive, but it is perhaps one of the few times we love with a pure love. Our heart may still feel the smarting pain from the offense, but when our neighbor says he is sorry and we forgive him from our heart, then we are saying, "I love you."

If the offense is repeated over and over, and time after time forgiveness is sought, then our love must always be there to stand tall as a rod near a broken reed, upholding and encouraging.

Jesus never gave anyone up. He called Judas "friend" in the Garden of Olives and asked the Father to forgive those who crucified Him because they did not know what they were doing.

Jesus made a distinction between an offense and His reaction to that offense. He somehow separated the two by love. When we are offended, we become so one with the offense that it possesses our souls and obliterates from our minds every other thought.

We eat, sleep, and drink the offense, our spirits become rebellious, our souls disturbed, our minds resentful. We become what our thoughts are, and our lives become a nightmare.

We don't see this in Jesus, and we cannot gloss over this fact by saying that He was God after all! He came for the purpose of giving us an example to live by, and we must find out how He did what He did.

His love for His enemies was greater than their malice. His love for His Apostles was greater than their weaknesses. His love for sinners was greater than their sins; His love for the poor greater than their need. His love for the sick was greater than the ingratitude many manifested when the gift of health was restored.

Throughout His life His love was always greater than the pain inflicted upon Him by His creatures. Perhaps this is where we fail. Our love is often less or not very far above an offense. The constant rehearsing of our neighbors' weaknesses in the

Playhouse of our Memory soon drains our heart of love and our Will of perseverance.

Our love soon runs dry unless we attach ourselves to that unlimited source of love—Jesus. Our love is not as strong as our tendency toward resentment and anger. If it were, we would take advantage of every occasion to practice virtue and imitate Jesus.

If we desire our love to grow stronger, then we must be willing to wait, to endure, to forgive, and to forget.

There are times, however, when love takes a strange turn. What do we do with those who do not injure us personally but whose weaknesses cause grave scandal? Jesus answers this dilemma by saying, "If your brother does something wrong, go and have it out with him alone, between your two selves." This encounter with an erring brother is an act of love because it is done in private. Concern for the individual causes us to go to him and kindness makes us want to correct him alone without the embarrassment of witnesses. It is love then that moves our will to act and act kindly. "If he listens to you, you have won back your brother," Jesus assures us (Matt. 18:15).

However, "if he does not listen, take one or two others along with you; the evidence of two or three witnesses is required to sustain any charge" (Matt. 18:16). Love is undaunted. It is possible that our individual personality clouded our reason in our efforts to correct our brother; it is then necessary to procure the help of others more knowledgeable to aid us in leading a straying brother back to the fold.

If this persevering love has no effect, Jesus gives us the next step, by saying, "if he refuses to listen, report it to the community, and if he refuses to listen to the community, treat him like a pagan or a tax collector" (Matt. 18:17). Those who were listening to Jesus knew perfectly well what He meant. A pagan or a tax collector was an outcast. He was excommunicated from the Temple and could not enter until the priests of the Temple gave their permission for him to do so. This permission was given only upon the acceptance of the one and only God in the case of a pagan, and a complete change of life in the case of a tax collector.

The same would hold true in the New Covenant. Jesus ended this instruction by saying to His Apostles, "I tell you solemnly, whatever you bind on earth shall be bound in Heaven; whatever you loose on earth shall be loosed in Heaven" (Matt. 18:18).

This was the second time Jesus had made the statement about the power to bind and loose on earth. When Peter made his profession of faith in the Divinity of Jesus, he was told he was the Rock on which Jesus would build His Church. It was at that time Jesus gave Peter and all the Apostles the power to bind and loose. "So I now say to you: You are Peter and on this Rock I will build My Church. And the gates of the underworld can never hold out against it. I will give you the keys of the Kingdom of Heaven: whatever you bind on earth shall be considered bound in Heaven; whatever you loose on earth shall be considered loosed in Heaven" (Matt. 16:18-20).

Not everyone desires forgiveness for an offense or has the determination or will to change his life. Sin becomes such a way of life that all the pleading and reasoning in the world has no influence over them. This kind of person is not lost completely, for while there is a single breath left in his body there is hope of salvation. God's love will continue to pursue and hound him in order to turn him away from evil.

The fact remains, however, that one impenitent sinner, one hardened in sin, one person who enjoys evil, can influence weaker souls to the same sins. Love for the individual sinner and the community demands some kind of separation until that individual has changed his life.

In the natural order we separate a person with smallpox from society to keep the infection under control. Anyone with a highly infectious disease must be kept outside the community for two reasons. The first is for the sake of the sick person himself. Isolation enables him to regain his health. The second reason is the protection of the weak and the strong from contagion. This is also true in the supernatural order. Any individual who proves himself incorrigible or persists in a life of sin cannot be allowed to participate in the life of the Church. The Church cannot condone his evil.

We see this binding and loosing in the early Church. The Corinthians had in their midst a man guilty of incest. St. Paul's anger blazed when he heard of this sin. His condemnation was strong and swift. After reprimanding the community for not expelling such a man he said, "Though I am far away in body, I am with you in spirit, and have already condemned the man who did this thing as if I were actually present" (1 Cor. 5:3-4).

Here Paul is exercising a special power given to him by Jesus to loose and bind. "When you are assembled together in the name of the Lord Jesus, and I am spiritually with you, then with the power of our Lord Jesus he is handed over to Satan so that his sensual body may be destroyed and his spirit saved on the day of the Lord" (1 Cor. 5:4-5). Paul reminded them that this power to loose and bind was the power of Jesus, not his own. As a minister of that power, Paul was publicly expelling the guilty man from the entire Christian community. This punishment was to be administered during their community service so all would know this action was taken by the Power of Jesus given to Paul.

However, love was the root of what seemed on the surface a harsh punishment. The action was taken to make the man aware of the grievous sin he had committed and help him become more conscious of its gravity. The fact that the perpetrator of this evil act was a Christian made it more serious. If such a man were not publicly punished, his actions would be taken as something acceptable to the Church.

Paul made it clear that it was not possible for a Christian to disassociate himself from every immoral person in the world. "To do that," he told them, "you would have to withdraw from the world altogether." No, it was the scandalous life of a brother Christian that they must disassociate themselves from. "You should not associate with a brother Christian who is leading an immoral life, or is a usurer, or idolatrous, or a slanderer or a drunkard or is dishonest; you should not even eat a meal with people like that" (1 Cor. 5:10-11).

If Christians today were to stay away from fellow Christians who lied, cheated, got drunk, or were immoral, our list of friends would be greatly reduced. Yes, the saddest commentary in the world today is the realization that there is little difference between pagans and Christians.

The man who was excommunicated from the community committed a sin that most pagans would not have committed. This was a scandal. The realization that one who did not know Jesus was capable of terrible sins was understandable, for without Him we can accomplish nothing good. To see a fellow Christian commit such a sin, a person in whom the Spirit of God took up His dwelling place, was inexcusable. The choice made by the man was not reasonable. To satisfy his lust he drove from his soul the very Presence of God. He chose himself over God and the Community. The Community had no choice but to leave the man to himself.

It was a visible example of the existence of hell. The soul rejected God, ceased to love the Community in which he lived by grieving it, and thereby cut himself off from love and peace. Fortunately, the man was repentant, for we read in Second

Corinthians, "The punishment already imposed by the majority on the man in question is enough; and the best thing now is to give forgiveness and encouragement, or he might break down from so much misery. So I am asking you to give some definite proof of your love for him" (2 Cor. 2:6-8).

In this one incident we see Paul binding and loosing, imposing punishment and releasing the punishment. He did this "through the Power of Jesus" in him, and he did it out of love for the man and for the Community. Love demanded his concern, punished in order to give light, and totally forgave when repentance was evident. Like Jesus, Paul loved his brother enough to do what was best for him at the moment.

We, too, must have the courage to impose punishment when justice demands retribution, and mercy when repentance follows sin. Love is not always sweet, but it should always be strong and persevering—willing to wait for improvement and soften the blow of justice.

This incident had been the cause of great anxiety in the Community of Corinth. Paul's anger, justice, and mercy had stirred the hearts and minds of many Christians. Some questioned his sincerity and felt abandoned by his apparent disfavor. Paul hastened to assure them that he loved them all. "When I wrote to you, in deep distress and anguish of mind, and in tears," he explained, "it was not to make you feel hurt but to let you know how much love I have for you" (2 Cor. 2:4).

We can be sure the Corinthians found it hard to realize that Paul's love for them was the cause of his anger. In the heartache of every reprimand there is love, even though our pain blocks out any tenderness expressed.

If we could see love behind the rebuke of a friend, then our humiliation would be less and our humility greater. We would see love expressing itself in vehement concern!

Humble and Faithful Love

A Faithful Love is a reliable love—a love that can be counted on. There are many souls who find it difficult to express love, but when a friend is in need they are always the first to help. Their love, seemingly unemotional, is nonetheless faithful.

It requires deep spiritual insight to see in others the particular kind of love they are capable of expressing, and it takes a humble heart to be satisfied with that kind of love.

Being faithful is not only loving much and always; it is also gratefully receiving love from others. Most people find joy in giving but find it difficult to receive. They are awkward in their gratitude when they are the beneficiaries of any charity or kindness.

Perhaps we are too proud to receive because we are so condescending when we give. A humble love is content to give even when that giving is unappreciated and to receive when necessity makes one reach out for help.

Love brings with it peace and joy, and only the man with a humble heart can hope to find any kind of lasting peace and love. When Jesus asked us to be "gentle and humble of heart" and promised we would "find rest for our souls" He was telling us that a humble love is content merely to give.

A humble love "does not find fault" because it is more aware of the beam in its own eye than the splinter in its brother's eye" (1 Cor. 13:4-7).

A humble love is "never boastful or conceited." It thinks more of the accomplishments of others than its own and is ever aware of its limitations.

A humble love is "never rude or selfish" and yet we seldom think of someone who is polite and generous to us, saying, "I love you."

A humble love "never takes offense" because it does not judge the motive of other people's actions.

A humble love is "never resentful" because it is nourished by opportunities to forgive.

A humble love "grieves over the sins" of the world and is ever mindful of the weaknesses of human nature.

A humble love is always ready to excuse the faults of others because it is conscious of its own weaknesses.

A humble love "trusts" even though it is disappointed and offended by deceit.

A humble love never loses "hope" because its source is a provident Father who takes care of His own.

A humble love will "endure" any trial, heartache, pain, or tragedy because it sees the hand of God in every event.

Anyone who loves in any of the above ways loves deeply. Words may fail him for special occasions, but down deep in the heart of that individual is a faithful, humble love that is constant, persevering, and strong.

Only a humble and faithful love can continue when a loved one strays from the path of God. It takes great courage and stamina to continue loving one who rejects every effort to change and stubbornly adheres to a life of sin. But a humble love will continue to pray and love even when communication and dialogue are impossible.

A humble, faithful love is content to love from afar, wait with patience, and forgive at the least sign of repentance.

God Himself loves through a humble heart, for that heart "delights in truth" and the truth searches the hearts of others and brings out everything that is good.

No Greater Love

"Yes, God loved the world so much that He gave His only Son" (John 3:16). The Father manifested His great love for us by sacrifice. Jesus proved His love for the Father also by sacrifice. The effect of God's love for mankind was sacrifice and suffering. It cost Him to show us His love, and it cost Jesus to show the Father His love for Him and mankind.

"The Father loves Me because I lay down my life in order to take it up again." Jesus was commanded by the Father to die for all men, and the love of Jesus acquiesced to that plan. "I lay it down" He told the Pharisees "of My own free will, and as it is in My power to lay it down, so it is in My power to take it up again; and this is the command I have been given by My Father" (John 10:17-18).

The effect of the love of the Father and Son both for each other and mankind was sacrifice. True love is proven, tried, and strengthened by the readiness and capability to sacrifice.

God expects us, in fact commands us, to love our neighbor in the same way He loves us. As His love for us was manifested by sacrifice, so our love for Him and our neighbor must be manifested by sacrifice. "Unless a wheat grain fall on the ground and die it remains only a single grain.... Anyone who loves his life loses it; anyone who hates his life in this world will keep it for eternal life" (John 12:24-25).

The ability to sacrifice is the tiny seed planted in our hearts by a loving God. We are able constantly to discern between the things that last and the things that pass. We are detached enough to do with or to do without and find peace with either one.

Surface love, the kind built on emotions and appearances, cannot survive for long because it lacks the proper ground in which to grow. It is like a plant with shallow roots—blown away by the least wind of adversity.

The Enemy encourages any love whose roots are pleasure, selfish gain, and self-interest. He knows that this kind of love will one day turn to hate, and the father of hate can give only what he possesses.

God's love, on the contrary, is rooted in sacrifice, and He desires our love to be as strong and unfaltering as His love. We must not only possess that love, but we must ever remain in that love. Here again, it is a spirit of sacrifice that enables us to do so.

"If you keep My Commandments," Jesus told His followers, "you will remain in my love." Is there anyone who can deny the fact that keeping those Commandments requires self-control, self-discipline, and a spirit of sacrifice?

Jesus assured us that He would call us "friends" on one condition. "You are My friends," He said, "if you do what I command you" (John 15:14). And what does Jesus command us to do?

We read in the Gospel of St. John, "I give you a new Commandment, love one another just as I have loved you" (John 13:34). The love of Jesus for us was one great sacrifice from the moment of His Incarnation to His death, and though His Goodness strews our path with many joys—still, our love for Him is proven by our fidelity in time of stress and pain.

- Love is not proven by feeling good but by being good.
- Love is not made stronger in consolation but in desolation.
- Love does not see everything through rose-colored glasses but makes all bitter things sweet.
- Love ever seeks to be generous but is satisfied only when it is noble.
- Love feels the searing pangs of rejection but never permits the pain to extinguish its own fire.
- Love is never satisfied with its own way of expression but is overjoyed at the least sign of love from others.
- Love is never concerned as to how others return love. Love only wants to love.

No End

There is in every book a final chapter to sum up the author's conclusions, solve a problem, or prove a point, but when we speak of love and the ways each human being expresses that gift from God, there is truly no way to end the book.

Every man must take the Father as an example of "how" to love. He must take Jesus as an example of "expressing" love, and then open his soul to the Holy Spirit who is Love, in order to "give" love to his neighbor.

When we give the Holy Spirit free reign to love in us, we will be extremely sensitive as to how others are expressing their love to us. It is then that we will love as He loves—freely; forgive as He forgives—without limit; and be ready to give up all things for His sake.

Jesus My Savior

"It is never the will of your Father in heaven that one of these little ones should be lost" (Matt. 18:14).

God's Will is that we are all saved — that we imitate Jesus in our daily lives, that we accomplish His holy and perfect Will, that we see His Providence in the present moment, and that we love our neighbor in the way He loves him. When we prefer our will to His, we sin or weaken our will.

By His life, death, and Resurrection Jesus merited the indwelling of the Spirit [in us] and through the grace of His Spirit, we are able to rise above our own will and desires and live in His Will, His peace, and His love.

We have then two aspects of Salvation: God's and ours.

God's Will

- ☙ The Father wills that we be saved.
- ☙ Jesus merited salvation by shedding His Precious Blood.

- The Spirit fills our souls with grace—gifts and fruits in order to sanctify us.

Our Cooperation

- We must want to be saved and use this desire by doing the Father's Will.
- We must utilize the fruits of Redemption by sorrow for sin, reception of the Eucharist, Baptism, Confession, Confirmation, and the other sacraments as our state in life requires.
- We must be faithful to the Church; grow in Faith, Hope, and Love; change our lives; and make Jesus known as Lord by living saintly lives.

The Trinity desires each one of us to be saved, but unless we accept that salvation by humble repentance and loving adherence to His Will, we cannot obtain salvation.

The unforgivable sin that Jesus spoke of is the refusal to admit one's guilt before God. God cannot forgive a sinner who does not acknowledge his sin. There exist two opposite wills—God requires repentance so He may forgive, while the sinner refuses to admit anything to be forgiven. There is created a spiritual impasse that can end in the soul's eternal rejection of God.

There are many who believe that the acceptance of Jesus as Savior is sufficient to be saved, but Jesus assures us that this is not so. "It is not those who say to me, 'Lord, Lord,' who will enter the Kingdom of Heaven, but the person who does the will of My Father in heaven" (Matt. 7:21). Here we find a condition attached to salvation, and that condition is that we do the Father's Will.

We must be found secure in that Will when we are called, for Jesus reminds us that "the man who stands firm to the end will be saved" (Matt. 10:22). We are not to be presumptuous in regard to salvation. We cannot put off a change of life for tomorrow or old age, for there may be no tomorrow. Jesus died for our sins, but that death did not give us license to commit sin. His death merited the indwelling of His own Spirit into our souls. This indwelling makes us Temples of God. We carry His Divine Presence within us everywhere we go. St. Paul told the Corinthians, "Examine yourselves to make sure you are in the faith; test yourselves. Do you acknowledge that Jesus Christ is really in you? If not, you have failed the test" (2 Cor. 13:5).

Sin defiles the Temple of our souls; it makes it a "den of thieves." To continue a life of sin while one confesses Jesus is Lord is hypocrisy, for Jesus is not Lord of the Temple from whose portal comes evil — this is blasphemy.

God's grace is at its best in weakness, so we need never fear our weakness. In fact, these weaknesses will determine in what way we shall glorify God for all eternity. As we overcome those qualities and traits in our souls that are not Christ-like, we acquire more of the likeness of Jesus. This is the process of holiness — constant growth through quick, humble repentance. The true Christian has a moral certainty that God's mercy will always be extended to him. He realizes that God is his Father and that loving Father will do everything possible to assure a place for His son in His Kingdom. The uncertain aspect of salvation is not on the part of God, but on the part of the creature.

We are to have an unfailing hope in the mercy of God in our regard and a humble attitude of heart that is prudently cautious of ourselves. Self-knowledge makes us realize it is necessary to be vigilant, and St. Peter warns us, "Be calm but vigilant, because your enemy the devil is prowling round like a roaring lion, looking for someone to eat" (1 Pet. 5:8).

Peter knew from experience that even after confessing with his lips that Jesus was the Son of God, even after being with

Jesus, even after having been given the Keys of the Kingdom, it was possible to fall deeply. Except for his loving and repentant heart, Peter might have ended like Judas. Throughout the Scriptures we see a holy, prudent caution — coupled with a confident trust in God as merciful Father. God and the soul cooperate together and become united in heart and mind.

To believe one may continue living a sinful life and still be saved by a semblance of lip service is deception. Jesus warned us when He said, "Many false prophets will arise; they will deceive many … but the man who stands firm to the end will be saved" (Matt. 24:11, 13). Here we find the necessity of not succumbing to the false prophets of our day and the promise of salvation at the end of life.

The word "salvation" means "to be saved from, to be delivered from." This is what Jesus merited for us by His death and Resurrection. The power of His Spirit endowed us with grace to withstand the onslaughts of the enemy, rise above our worldly desires, and overcome our weaknesses. Jesus reconciled us with the Father. We are a forgiven people, a people who belong to their God in a father-son relationship. His home is our home, His love is our love, His mercy is our mercy. Everything He is by nature, He gives us by grace. This raises us far above anything we had before redemption, for now we are heirs to the Kingdom, sons of God, children of the Father.

All of this is salvation here and now. It culminates in our entering the Kingdom to be forever happy with the Trinity. Salvation is a growth experience, a constant changing of attitudes, ideas, goals, and desires, an awareness of the invisible realities, a life of Faith in His Promises, Hope in His grace, and Love of our neighbor.

Salvation is not a ticket to Heaven that is used at death. A soul cannot go his way, living a life away from God, alienated from His Spirit, and then suddenly be caught up into the Arms of God because of a belief that bore no fruit. Deathbed conversions are possible, but it is presumptuous to put off living a Christian life until then.

Every moment of life is important, and we see Paul using every occasion to increase grace and assure his salvation. On one occasion he was told of some who were preaching the Good News with selfish motives. Paul answered this complaint with humble patience. His answer was that he was happy to hear Christ proclaimed no matter what the motive "because I know this will help to save me, thanks to your prayers and to the help which will be given to me by the Spirit" (Phil. 1:18-19). To

Paul, salvation was a change of life, and that change continued and grew out of every minute of his life.

The need to persevere in our quest for salvation was brought out very clearly by Jesus. He explained the condition of a man who was delivered from an unclean spirit. His soul was in a state of grace. However, the evil spirit, who had once inhabited that soul, sought out other spirits more evil than himself and once more took up his abode. Presumption, complacency, and negligence had opened the door "so that the man ended up by being worse than he was before" (Luke 11:24, 26). Similarly, in the parable of the seed, Jesus brings out clearly how some hear the word and accept it with joy—salvation has entered their hearts. But trials, persecution, money, riches, and worries choke that word and they fall away (Matt. 13:22).

Over and over again Jesus repeats the admonition to persevere to the end—to that moment when He calls and at which time we will see the fruit we have borne. "You and I," Paul told the Hebrews, "are not the sort of people who draw back and are lost, we are the sort who keep faithful until our souls are saved" (Heb. 10:39).

St. John told his followers one day, "our love is not to be just words or mere talk, but something real and active; only by this can we be certain that we are children of truth ... because we keep His commandments and live the kind of life that He wants" (1 John 3:18, 22).

Those who have accepted the salvation Jesus merited for them should possess freedom, not from temptation, but from the tyranny of the world, the flesh, and the devil. It is grace that gives us the courage and strength to consistently fight against these three enemies of the soul. As we grow in this freedom we take on more and more of Jesus. We are light in the darkness for others to see by; we are cities on top of the mountain, beckoning the people of God to rise to greater heights.

Faith enables us to see God in everything and everyone. Hope enables us to see God bringing good out of everything, and Love enables us to respond to the virtue of the Moment with joy. This is salvation at work—working and growing until it enjoys the perfect freedom of the sons of God in His Kingdom. It is ever active, and seeking ways of becoming stronger, for salvation is a way of life.

Salvation brings the soul a deep awareness of God's love. Life takes on more meaning for it now has a purpose. Trials and crosses are no longer mysteries but caresses from the

Crucified Lord. Worldly ambition is changed to a thirst and hunger for holiness. Riches are neither desired nor abhorred for neither poverty embitters, nor riches distract the soul from its only love.

Like Paul, the soul is always aware that it is merely "an earthenware jar," but the Blood of Jesus has given it a "power that comes from God alone" (2 Cor. 4:7). When a man of the world looks at those who have experienced the freedom of salvation, he sees Christians who often have "difficulties on every side but are never cornered; they see no answer to their problems but never despair; they are persecuted but never deserted; knocked down but never killed." Yes they "carry in their body the death of Jesus so the life of Jesus may be seen in their body" (2 Cor. 4:8-10).

There was no doubt that Paul took salvation seriously and as an everyday encounter. "Indeed, while we are still alive, we are consigned to our death every day, for the sake of Jesus, so that in our mortal flesh the life of Jesus may be openly shown" (2 Cor. 4:11).

The Christians of our time are to prove to the world that they belong to God; God is their Father. They prove this by "fortitude in times of suffering, in times of hardship and

279

distress; by purity, knowledge, patience, kindness and a spirit of holiness." They are truly free for they are ready "for honor or disgrace, blame or praise," success or failure, riches or poverty, health or sickness.

St. Peter tells us that our hope in His promises are sure and we should not be surprised if our faith is tested as in a fire (1 Pet. 1:3-9). "You are sure," he says, "of the end to which your faith looks forward, that is, the salvation of your souls." And yet, in Peter as in Paul we find a holy caution. "If anyone," he says, "who has escaped the pollution of the world once by coming to know Our Lord and Savior Jesus Christ, and who then allows himself to be entangled by it a second time and mastered, will end up in a worse state then he began in" (2 Pet. 2:20). We realize that Salvation, which is an active participation in the grace of the Spirit in our daily lives, is a gift from God. He gives us a share in His Divine Nature as a free gift, and yet, He expects us to use another gift—free will—and deliberately choose to follow Him, love Him, and prefer Him to ourselves. He desires to forgive us but He must hear our repentance and see our efforts to change.

St. John puts down certain conditions that are necessary on our part (1 John).

- First: Break with sin (Ch. 1 & 3).
- Second: Keep the commandments, especially the commandment to love (Ch. 2 & 3).
- Third: Detachment from the world (Ch. 2).
- Fourth: Be on guard against false prophets (Ch. 2 & 3).

This may give the impression that the soul does it all, but St. John solves our dilemma by telling us that if we acknowledge our sins, God will forgive us because Jesus is the sacrifice that takes our sins away. He tells us that "we can be sure we are in God only when we live the same kind of life as Christ lived." He assured us that "nothing the world has to offer, the sensual body, the lustful eye, or pride in possessions, could ever come from God but only from the world."

To John, the discerning of false prophets was an easy matter. He promised that the Spirit of Jesus in us would make us recognize false prophets for "the world listens to them, but we are children of God and those who know God listen to us; those who are not of God refuse to listen" (1 John 4:6).

Does this mean only Christians will be saved, will enter His Kingdom? No, Holy Mother Church has always taught that all men are given enough light to enter the Kingdom, but they enter there through the Blood of Jesus; they belong to the soul of the Church, and at death God will judge them according to the light they possessed. We shall not all be judged by the same standards, for Jesus assures us, "The servant who knows what his master wants but has not even started to carry out those wishes, will receive very many strokes of the lash. The one who did not know, but deserves to be beaten for what he has done, will receive fewer strokes. When a man has had a great deal given him, a great deal will be demanded of him; when a man has had a great deal given him on trust, even more will be expected of him" (Luke 12:47-48). Here are four definite degrees of light given by God to His children, and each is required to produce accordingly. The person who knew God and did nothing about it, the one who did not know God, the one given much light, and the priest or minister who was given more than he needed for himself in order to share it with others. Each will be judged according to the light received and how he used it.

Jesus not only told us we would all be judged differently; He also gave us some definite conditions for entering the Kingdom. Each of the following conditions was proclaimed in a solemn manner so we would be aware of the importance of what He said.

Solemn Proclamations

I tell you solemnly, unless a man is born from above … unless he is born through water and the Spirit, he cannot enter the Kingdom. (John 3:5)

I tell you solemnly, if you do not eat the Flesh of the Son of Man and drink His Blood, you will not have life in you. (John 6:53)

I tell you solemnly, unless you change and become like little children, you will never enter the Kingdom of Heaven. (Matt. 18:3)

These solemn proclamations show us the necessity of a constant growth in the spiritual life. God Himself effects this growth with His Grace and Presence through the Sacraments, Commandments, Scripture, and good works. This change that our neighbor perceives in our daily lives, manifests our Faith, Hope, and Love. We need not speak of salvation for it is apparent to everyone that we have been saved from the tyranny of the Enemy and, as such, enjoy the freedom of the Sons of God, for our lives portray the Love and virtues of Jesus.

"It is to the glory of My Father that you should bear fruit and then you will be my disciples" (John 15:8). This is salvation in action — this separates the children of Light from the children of darkness — this is reaping the fruit of Redemption.

THE GOOD LIFE

THE GIFT OF LIFE: HE
CHOSE ME TO BE

"Before I formed you in the womb I knew you" (Jer. 1:5). Our minds cannot comprehend how special each soul is to God. We do not understand the dignity that is ours when His Goodness chose each one of us to live, to think, to know, to see, to love.

We did not happen to be — we were chosen by God to exist. Before time began God chose each one of us, and this choice was deliberate. God saw all the possible human beings He might have created throughout the history of the world. Out of possible billions of human beings that might have existed in God's mind — His Eye rested on each one of us and then stopped looking and said, "You shall be." He saw all who could have been and decided they would not be. His providence placed us in a time and state of life that would bring out our greatest potential.

He gave each of us special talents, gifts, and natural virtues all geared towards a deeper knowledge of Himself. Even those whose circumstances prevent them from knowing Him directly possess a deep conviction of His existence and providence.

He placed into each of us an inner radar system that warns of danger and assures us intuitively of His care, so we will never be far from Him and will not be deprived of the knowledge of His existence.

The Hand that formed each of us left Its imprint upon our minds and souls, for He made us to His own image. The soul He breathed into this work of His Hands — our body — was imprinted with some of His love — His creative power — His strength.

We reflect His eternity, for once His Will called us out of nothingness, we became immortal — our soul will never die.

"Yahweh called me before I was born, from my mother's womb he pronounced my name" (Isa. 49:1).

We read in the Gospel of St. John that when Jesus appeared to Mary Magdalen she thought He was the gardener.

Her mind was not ready for the Resurrection, and then she heard her name — "Mary!" Was it the tone of voice that made her recognize Jesus, or was it because the God-Man pronounced it? Did it perhaps have the resounding quality of an echo as it reached her ears? That name was pronounced by God before she was born — before time began. At its sound a creature awoke, first out of nothingness, then out of sin, and now out of sorrow. The first time it was pronounced, her birth was decreed; the second time, she came to be; the third time, it called her to rebirth; and now, after the Resurrection, it called her to recognize her God in Spirit, in herself, in her neighbor, and in faith. When man pronounces a name, it is mostly a call to serve, but when God pronounces it, it bestows life, power, grace, and joy. When Jesus said, "Lazarus come forth," a dead man arose; when He changed the name of Simon to Peter he gave a specific mission and power to a man. When He thundered, "Saul, Saul, why do you persecute Me?" a man was struck blind, transformed, and called by the name Paul. How wonderful and how fortunate we are as God constantly calls our name and bestows upon us the grace to change and respond to His love.

"You drew me out of the womb, you entrusted me to my mother's breasts; placed on your lap from birth, from my mother's womb you have been my God" (Ps. 22:9-10).

The psalmist realizes that it was the Lord God who held him in His lap as his natural mother fed and cared for him. He saw God upholding his body, giving him strength and all the necessary bodily functions to grow. We must never lose sight of this reality. Never for a moment has God ceased caring, providing for, and loving us. Even at those times when others seemed to have charge of our growth and care — it was done so on the lap of God — the loving care of a compassionate Father, Who never ceased to look after us. He did so in such silence that we were not aware of His concern. It was as if His power might frighten us or His strength crush us, that He handled our formation and growth with such tenderness and silence. It is unfortunate that we have mistaken silence for absence and tenderness for neglect.

"You know me through and through, from having watched my bones take shape when I was being formed in secret, knitted together in the limbo of the womb" (Ps. 139:15).

Only God knows us as we are. When the Psalmist said God knows us through and through, he meant every aspect of our creation, life, talents, temperament, and characteristics. He knew the crosses that would come our way and how each one would help to change, mold, and form our soul to His Image. Like all fathers, He looked forward to the day He would see Himself clearly mirrored in us. He anticipated our choosing Him above all things and saw what marvelous glory those choices would give us. He saw the holiness we might obtain, the humility of heart that would be like a shield around us. He saw the tears His love would gently wipe away and the times He would lean down to take hold of our hand as we fell from grace. He saw our bad choices and grieved over our pain and then sought ways to bring good out of everything. Yes, He knew us then, through and through, as He knows us now and—still He loves us.

"My days were listed and determined even before the first of them occurred" (Ps. 139:16).

We have such a low opinion of ourselves: our sense of God's justice is so severe, our comprehension of His mercy is meager, our delight in His love short-lived. We reserve our expression of love for God as an act of gratitude after some favor has been received. How often do we think of God's love for us before one day of our existence came into being? With what love and care He brought us forth and determined the length of our days! We did not just happen to be. We have a mission to fulfill, a place in His Kingdom to occupy, a duty to perform and a work to accomplish. We are important to God and an integral part of salvation history. Each human being exerts an influence, changes people for good or bad, builds or destroys, uses or creates opportunities. We can truthfully say each human being changes the world for good or bad and the world is not the same because each one of us has lived in it. No matter how insignificant our role, how lowly our position, how unknown our contribution, each one of us leaves a mark somewhere, in some way upon this world. No wonder He chooses us with great care and determines our course with infinite love. What a gift is life!

"The Holy Spirit will come upon you," the angel answered Mary, "and the power of the Most High will cover you with its shadow." "I am the handmaid of the Lord ... let what you have said be done to me" (Luke 1:35, 38).

What marvels and mysteries God wraps up in short paragraphs. The whole world waited, studied, discerned, fasted, and prayed for the coming of the Holy One. The account of His Incarnation is short, but filled with food for thought. God sent an angel to ask Mary to consent to being the Mother of the Redeemer. He respects the powerful gift He has given us. He would not perform this wonder of wonders without her consent. The angel told her not to fear—her virginity would be secure—it was the Holy Spirit, enveloping this beautiful Temple of the Lord, who would say, "Let the Word be made Flesh." The same Voice that hovered over the void and said, "Let there be light" would bring forth the Eternal Word and place It in the cradle of Mary's womb. The moment her will concurred with the Father's Will, the Word was made Flesh and dwelt among us.

There are many opinions today as to when a seed becomes a person—a human being—a nature with powers to decide and to accomplish. When is a soul implanted into the body of a developing human being? Some say when the heart begins to beat, others when brain waves begin to function. What does Scripture say? What visible proof do we possess to solve this mystery?

We know that "Jesus was like us in all things but sin." We must see if the Incarnate Word in the womb of the Immaculate Temple of God—Mary—was fruitful, powerful, alive, a Divine Person: God-Man. Scripture tells us the angel Gabriel had informed Mary that her cousin Elizabeth had conceived a son in her old age. Immediately after the announcement of her own Motherhood, "Mary set out at that time and went as quickly as she could to a town in the hill country of Judah." We are speaking here of a long journey—a journey made by a woman who had just said her "Amen" to God. There was no doubt in her mind that she immediately possessed and carried in her womb the Son of God.

So evident was the Divine Presence within her—so powerful and strong that tiny seed—that as soon as she greeted her cousin Elizabeth, the child Elizabeth carried experienced the power of the Word made Flesh. Elizabeth and her six-month-old child felt the Presence of the One who called them forth from nothingness. The God-Man, who had been placed just one day before in the darkness of Mary's Immaculate womb, gave the light of holiness and sanctifying grace to His living but unborn Precursor. Mother and child felt a Presence and their souls felt drawn, humbled, and joyful. "Elizabeth gave a loud cry and said, 'Of all women you are the most blessed, and blessed is the fruit of your womb. Why should I be honored with a visit from the mother of my Lord?'" (Luke 1:42-43). It was certainly a mystery to Elizabeth. The Incarnate Son of God began redeeming mankind and spreading the Good News as soon as He was made Flesh.

At the time of the Incarnation, Elizabeth was in her sixth month, and Luke informs us that Mary stayed with her for three months—until the birth and circumcision of John the Baptist. There is no question that Mary began that visit immediately after the Word was made Flesh. There can now be no question in our minds as to when the soul and body are united to form a being made to the image and likeness of God. It is at conception.

If there were in Mary merely the beginning of a body without a human soul united to Divinity there would have been no reaction on the part of Elizabeth and her unborn son—no exclamation of surprise at the honor of being visited and cared for by God's own Mother. Motherhood surely begins when there is a whole being within a woman, a being with a body and a soul united together to form a human person. Elizabeth attested to the reality of this truth by calling Mary the Mother of her Lord. She saw two mysteries in one intuitive glance — the Incarnation of the Messiah and the reality of a fully human person at conception.

When God says, "Let there be life," dare we say "It shall not be"?

"Your body, you know, is the temple of the Holy Spirit, who is in you since you received Him from God. You are not your own property; you have been bought and paid for. That is why you should use your body for the glory of God" (1 Cor. 6:19-20).

We have a tendency to think our body is our own and we can do as we please with it. But this is not so. We were created by God — created as weak human beings, part animal, part spiritual. Our dignity as human beings was degraded by pride and rebellion in the beginning by our first parents Adam and Eve and then by our own wrong choices. God's love for us devised a way to raise us above our degradation—above our own nature—and set us apart as beings He could rightfully call "sons." He sent His own Son to take our flesh upon Himself—live and die as one of us and then rise from the dead so we would be delivered from our slavery to sin. What a price was paid for one so fragile in nature, so vacillating in will, so prone to evil. The Great King looks for a peasant to raise up to the dignity of a Prince. Each one of us is a kind of Cinderella, who is beckoned by the King to live a new life. The choice is ours, but the prize is His—He has already a right to everything we are, everything we possess. He has only good to give us. Why do we so often prefer what harms us? Is the right to choose good and evil more precious to us than peace, happiness, and joy? Would we rather be miserable and misuse our freedom to choose rather than be humble and admit God knows what is best for us? What price He paid to save us and what price we pay when we do our own will? No, we do not have a right to do as we please with our life or anyone else's. Our life belongs to God, and that God is powerful enough to maintain it, good enough to sustain it, and provident enough to care for all its needs.

Our body, St. Paul says, houses the Spirit of the Lord. It is a Temple. To desecrate it by sin or to take away its life-giving spirit, is to commit an injustice to God, man, and oneself: to God because He created it and it belongs to Him; to our neighbor because he needs to see God radiate in our lives; and to ourselves because we were created to be sons of God and heirs to His Kingdom.

We forget that everything God created is good. The Book of Genesis assures us of this, for after each day's account it says God "saw that it was good." If this is true of inanimate and animal creation, how much more is it true of human beings — made to the image and likeness of God. Whatever is not good in our lives is our own doing most of the time, but even in circumstances such as these, God brings good out of it for us. The only evil in the world is sin, for sin destroys and kills, but God's grace raises up dead souls and makes them new by repentance, confession, and absolution. Once more God can say, "It is good — it is very good."

"Listen to me ... you who have been carried since birth, whom I have carried since the time you were born. In your old age I shall still be the same, when your hair is gray I shall still support you" (Isa. 46:4).

"You will be like a son of the Most High, whose love for you will surpass your mother's" (Ecclus. 4:11 [Sir. 4:10]).

"Like a son comforted by his mother will I comfort you" (Isa. 66:13).

"I, I am your consoler. How can you be afraid of mortal man, of the son of man, whose fate is the fate of grass?" (Isa. 51:12).

Yes, we do not appreciate the gift of life. We have lost the reality of God's care and love for us from conception to death. We look at nature as if this unintelligent work of God's hand decided our fate — the fate of intelligent beings. We look to the world for directions of thought and action. We look at our neighbor and try to measure up to his concepts and ideals. We look everywhere and anywhere for guidance and help, but we do not go to the Source of our life, the Cause of our being, the Dispenser of our intelligence, and the Life of our spirit.

Some look upon birth as an accident, life as a necessary evil, and death as resignation to the inevitable. The prospect can become so clouded by selfishness, statistics, and pride that a womb giving life is turned into a tomb of death. There are others whose concepts of life become so narrow, their future so hopeless, and their present so unbearable, that the only solution to their problem is the extinction of that life completely. And then there are many who live in a kind of nether-world—the darkness of inferiority—of uselessness, of despair without a thought of God, love, or of what is to come. They live within a circle of their own thoughts, selfish desires, and self-hatred. If only all those living in these painful, frustrating attitudes would realize how much they are loved by God, how they have a place in His plans, how He watches over them, cares for them, and desires they be with Him in His Kingdom. Surely the realization of being created, supported, loved, and cared for from conception, through life, and in death would secure freedom to the unborn, give courage to the destitute and confidence to the hopeless.

God has our entire lives in the palm of His loving Hands —we can rest secure about our past, present, and future for He loves us.

SYMPATHETIC GENEROSITY

In His Service

There is in the heart of every Christian the need to be of service to God and His Kingdom. We see a multitude of needs in the Church, in our Community, in our Parish, and in the world. The magnitude of these needs, however, often produces a paralyzing effect in us. As a result, we stand by and do nothing. The sick feel left out, the poor feel inadequate, the young inexperienced, the old incapacitated, and those in between, too busy. These attitudes encourage spiritual inertia and lethargy. Perhaps it is because we do not understand that we are not all expected to serve Him in the same manner.

There are many ways of serving God in our particular state of life. We mention some that are more general and apply to all walks of life. Among these services we can render are: time, talent, suffering, prayer, and material means. One of the most precious gifts God has given us is time. It is a gift that must be traded well. Our eternity may depend on how well it is used. It is a tool in our hands with which we carve the edifice in which we will live for all eternity.

Much of time is wasted. We sometimes speak of "killing time," and a conscious concentration on its existence creates monotony and boredom. When we are in pain it drags, and when joy is our portion it flies. It seems endless when we're waiting for something important to happen and very short when the sudden joy of a rising sun begins our day.

Some of us dread the thought of its termination and although we do not always know what to do with it, we wish it would never end. We prefer to use it, in its entirety, for our own interests. We do not like to think it is an invisible reality in the Hands of Another. It is a gift, and we must share it with our brother through the performance of good works. It is also necessary to give some of that time to God in prayer and in evangelization. As we feed the poor and clothe the naked we must not forget that these exterior works of mercy must stem from a compassionate heart and a Christ-like spirit within us. If our good works are not the fruit of a deep union with God, then it is merely a contest between the "haves" and "have-nots."

Using some of our time, be it ever so little, in "prayerful evangelization" is necessary to preserve our zeal and enthusiasm. It is also within the scope of everyone. One of the petitions of the Lord's Prayer is that the Father's kingdom will come. This particular plea takes on a special significance in today's world. The Kingdom of God on earth is a holy people living the Gospel, sharing each other's goods, problems, joys, and sorrows. It is a manifestation of the Presence of God in our midst. Unfortunately, the spirit of this world places many smoke screens before this ideal, and we find it almost impossible to retain the Father's plan as a goal in life. The counsels and precepts of the Gospel become mere philosophical ideologies and not possible, realistic ways of living. To sustain our enthusiasm and perseverance in our striving, we need the Church, the Sacraments, and an habitual prayer life. We cannot give what we do not possess. We cannot teach what we do not understand. We cannot give witness to the power of prayer if we never pray. We cannot sanctify our day if the thought of His Presence does not begin it.

Yes, it is necessary for each of us to care enough about the world we live in to spend some time every day in prayer for its salvation. The fruit of this prayer is action. Be holy, and those around you will become holy; give them His Word, and their knowledge will increase; give them His love, and their grace will abound.

Prayer and action enable us to utilize our talents in His service. Just as we give of our gift of time, so should we give of our special talents. We do not speak of great talents or extraordinary talents, but of common, everyday, and many times unnoticed talents. It is a talent to be able to comfort a sick friend; a talent to explain a truth; a talent to care for the aged; a talent to bake a cake and give it to a bereaved friend; a talent to lift a heavy burden by a smile or a pat on the shoulder; a talent to laugh and make others laugh; a talent to bring peace and hope to the despairing and desperate.

These talents, put into God's service, make Christianity believable to the unbeliever. Talents that are exercised in imitation of Jesus, to promote the Father's glory, go a long way to spread the Good News.

The ability to suffer patiently, in union with the sufferings of Jesus, is also a talent, a special gift that can give courage, strength, and faith to others.

The endurance of loneliness in union with the loneliness of Jesus during His earthly exile can obtain the grace of repentance for many souls who have strayed from their Father's house. There is hardly a person in the whole world who does not have something to give to God in some way. We are very consistent in our requests for favors from God, but we seldom seek ways and means of serving and giving to Him—giving of ourselves, our time, our talents, our suffering, and last of all a share in the material benefits He has bestowed on us.

Of all the gifts we can give to God perhaps the one most misused is the monetary gift. We give money many times because it is the easiest thing to give and our obligations are over. To some it is a tax-deductible item or a balm for a guilty conscience. We are confused as to how much to give, when to give, whom to give to, and why we should give at all. We find money hard to make and difficult to part with. As a result, we grumble when we give and wonder if the one we gave to doesn't end up better off than we are. We think tithing is outdated and Scripture quotations about giving cheerfully are part of a plot to place guilt on our shoulders. Some make us feel we should give until it hurts, and others encourage us to plant a seed that will be doubled.

We have lost sight of the only reason for giving anything at all—love. If love and gratitude and a sincere desire to share is not at the root of our giving, we can be assured it is of no value. "If I give away all that I possess, piece by piece,... but am without love it will do me no good at all" (1 Cor. 13:3). "This does not mean that to give relief to others you ought to make things difficult for yourselves; it is a question of balancing what happens to be your surplus now, against their present need, and one day they may have something to spare that will supply your own need" (2 Cor. 8:13-14).

A monetary gift is a service of love, not a contribution. Love should be our motive and a dependence on Divine Providence part of our gift. This dispels any arrogance on the part of those who can give or resentment on the part of those who must receive. Both are where they are to glorify God—one by giving, another by receiving.

Paul assures us that "doing this holy service is not only supplying all the needs of the saints, but it is also increasing the amount of thanksgiving that God receives" (2 Cor. 9:12). To give is to do and to serve. It is to manifest our sincerity and make others give glory to God for His providential care. It is to listen to His inspirations and respond with love. It is to trust in Him as His Wisdom guides our lives so we sometimes give and sometimes receive.

Generalities may impress us and even inspire us, but until we act upon them it is useless knowledge. The following aids are given as helps in encouraging you to give your neighbor many opportunities to thank God as He uses you to make His Divine Providence a visible reality.

SUGGESTIONS FOR SERVICE OF TIME

- Listen to your neighbor who tells you of his problems.
- Listen to a sick friend explain his illness.
- Wait patiently for doctors, dentists, red lights, etc.
- Give some time to the building of your parish morale and your pastor's hope.
- Take time to compliment your pastor on a good sermon or a job well done.
- Take time to praise the members of your family or fellow workers.
- Visit or send a card to a prisoner or someone in a nursing home.
- Spend a few minutes telling God how great He is — how beautiful is the world He made.
- Be thoughtful by anticipating the needs of others.

- Take time to listen patiently; speak gently and act prudently.
- Take time to think before you say or do anything that may offend others.
- Distribute leaflets and pamphlets to friends. Place them in churches, beauty parlors, doctors' offices, etc.
- Take time to explain the beautiful truths of your religion to others.
- Read to the blind; run errands for the sick and elderly.
- Shop for the crippled.
- Visit nursing and rehabilitation centers.
- Volunteer to work in your local hospital.
- Ask your pastor where he needs help the most.
- Read the Bible on a scheduled basis, daily or weekly.

SUGGESTIONS FOR SERVICE OF TALENT

- Use the good qualities God has given you, such as love, patience, generosity, etc., to benefit your neighbor. Giving them will increase them.
- Home talents such as cooking, baking, cleaning can be used to help the infirm, sick, and elderly.

- Offer your business ability to your pastor or friend to help those who may make wrong business decisions.
- Extend His Kingdom by offering whatever talent you possess to be used by your parish, missionary endeavors, etc.
- Music and art talents can cheer the lonely and elderly.
- Sewing talents can be used for the poor or friends and relatives.
- Teaching talents spread the Good News.
- A joyful spirit encourages others.
- A gentle spirit acquiesces to the desires of others.
- Organizational talent can be offered for parish and civic committees.
- Speaking talent can spread high ideals.
- Drive a shut-in to Sunday Mass or other parish activities.

SUGGESTIONS FOR SERVICE OF PRAYER AND SUFFERING
- Praise and thank God for His goodness to you.
- Speak to Him often during the day by sharing your joys and sorrows with Him.
- Pray for the salvation of souls and the extension of His Kingdom and the good of Holy Mother Church.

- Pray for the People of God and the souls of the departed.
- Offer your sorrows, pain, and frustrations to God as an offering of sacrifice for the salvation of souls.
- Spend some time every day in the Silent Presence of God as you ask Him to fill you with His Goodness.
- Strive to be holy—to be like Jesus in your particular state in life.
- Pray for more people to work in the harvest.
- Pray that the Lord deliver all Christians from evil.
- Pray for the leaders of the country and Church.
- Pray for confirming signs for all who preach the Gospel.
- Pray for friends, relations, and enemies.
- Pray for the Gifts and Fruits of the Spirit for all Christians.
- Pray for orphans, prisoners, lonely, and aged.
- Unite your suffering with the suffering of Jesus for the salvation of souls.
- Make a sacrifice of service.
- Pray for those who are in prisons and for their regeneration in Jesus.
- "Adopt" a priest and pray for him every day, that his ministry will transform the world.

⮞ Go to Mass and Communion as often as possible. Offer the Mass for the salvation and blessings of your family, friends, and neighbors.

SUGGESTIONS FOR SERVICE OF MONETARY GIFTS

⮞ Use the material blessings God has given you to support His work.

⮞ Pray and ask the Holy Spirit to inspire you in your monetary gift giving.

⮞ Have a definite apostolate or purpose for your gift.

⮞ Obtain Bibles and spiritual literature for free distribution.

⮞ Choose some missionary to support as he works for the Kingdom.

⮞ Save small change to be used for items like stamps, envelopes, etc. for missionary endeavors.

⮞ Give a spiritual book to a friend for an Anniversary or Birthday.

⮞ Support your parish and diocesan activities.

⮞ Establish a trust, endowment, or give a bequest to support the Lord's work.

⮞ Help sponsor a Catholic TV Program.

← Give generously to the annual Catholic Charity drives and other organized appeals.

Prayer for the Bearer of Good News
Father, Lord of all, let me be a bearer of Good News
by an example of a holy life and by utilizing some of my
talents and time for the extension of Your Kingdom.
Lord Spirit, give me zeal and enthusiasm for spreading the
wealth of spirituality in the Church. Let Her Sacraments
become my source of strength and grace to fill souls with
hope. Send me at least one soul today that I may tell him
the news of Your love. Let the name of Jesus come quickly
to my lips as I reach out to touch the hopeless, the poor,
and the sick. Let mercy spring forth from my heart at any
offense so the world will know You are a forgiving God.

I give You my sufferings today so many souls will find the
light. I give You my love that others will find the Way. I give
You my day that others may see the reflection of Your Face.

Help me, Lord Jesus, to change the world and build
Your Church.

THE FAMILY SPIRIT

We live in an age that stresses personal goals, careers, happiness, work, and religion. The emphasis is on the individual and how best that individual can satisfy himself. There are as many degrees and types of living, ideals, and morals as there are people. Since one of the common denominators is freedom to do as one pleases, there is very little to contrast. To this way of thinking, everyone is free to be and do whatever he pleases without causing anyone any harm. This state of animated blahs perpetuates only darkness, for light is kindled by a clash of ideas, from strong concepts of right and wrong, from leaders who are fearless and stand tall on the side of justice.

We do not find choices between good and evil thrust upon us today—only the confusion of half-truths, blatant evil disguised as part of modern living, and an indifference to sin called "tolerance" and "love." Self-satisfaction at everyone else's expense is considered a kind of fulfillment, and any reaction to the contrary is an infringement on personal freedom.

Married life has become to many a necessary burden, but a burden that is shed very easily. Faithfulness has become merely a biblical term no longer relevant or possible in an age of modern enlightenment. Adultery and fornication have passed from unfaithfulness and sin to an inability to love only one person and the fulfillment of one's basic needs. Children who are to be the fruit of love are considered mere accidents, financial burdens, consumers of the world's food supply, an infringement on personal freedom to utilize untapped talents that are destined to be forever buried. This, alas, is the thinking of the minority to the dismay of the disheartened majority.

Not every family suffers from all these evils. But perhaps it is safe to say that we are all tainted in some way with their effects. What can we do to correct these ills? Where do we start? Do we run away and hide in some remote area or will that hopeless spirit follow us wherever we go? Do we band together for mutual upbuilding and protection? What happens to the rest of mankind if we retreat? Are the problems facing us so gigantic that we are forced to stand still as we wait for the final blow? Do Christians form minority groups for protection, growth, and perseverance?

Perhaps we should look at the Gospels to see what Jesus had to say. Whatever we find must be applicable to every form of Family Living, to Christians and non-Christians, for we all share the same Father—we are all the work of His Hands. We must also keep in mind that the Family Spirit concept is at the core of every Christian and the goal of every person who seeks happiness and goodness in this life.

A family spirit is not always synonymous with family life. Bone of our bone and flesh of our flesh makes for brothers, sisters, and relatives, who may be as distant as strangers in a foreign land. The world will always be blest with families or it will become extinct. It is not always blest with a family spirit in the midst of its families. The result is that every facet of daily life is affected with selfishness, indifference, lack of respect, cruelty, and coldness.

The Family is at the root of all society and the Family Spirit is a special quality that feeds the Family with vigor and vitality. When that spirit is present, there is a desire to cling together in time of crisis, to sacrifice in time of need and strength to face the demands of communal living.

The spirit of a family relationship affects our entire lives, and we have suffered from the lack of that spirit on the communal, parish, and national level. In neighborhoods there is fear of murder and robbery. Over the fence chitchat is nonexistent, for the "personal living" concept has made us disinterested in our neighbor's welfare. We fear his burden will become ours, and we are little concerned with his heartache, loneliness, or suffering. The aged become merely another obstacle to surmount. Each home is only a house in which individuals live—alone together—in miniature motels. Neighbors are competitors instead of partners, suspicious instead of trustful, indifferent instead of helpful, cold instead of loving, greedy instead of generous. We no longer consider ourselves living in neighborhoods, but only as living next to "hoods." We live in wealthy, middle-class, or poor sections of a city, rather than communities of people living together for mutual growth.

As the individual family lives, so lives the immediate community, the parish, the city and state, the nation and the world. A countryside is ugly or beautiful according to the tiny seeds sown in abundance. From weeds come shocking overgrowth that is neither appealing nor inspiring, but from selected seeds, cared for and pruned during growth, come trees to delight the eye and fruit to nourish the body. Let us see what is lacking in our family living and its various aspects, why it is unsightly and distressing, why it has sunk to such depths in so short a time. Do the Gospels tell us what we can or cannot do? If so, let us look deeply to see if there is any solution to such a problem.

First, we know a few things we cannot do, and one of them is, we cannot run away. "I am not asking you to remove them from the world but to protect them from the evil one" (John 17:15). We are to change the world, transform it as we are transformed, renew its spirit as ours is renewed, and we are to do this in the midst of the wickedness in the world. "They do not belong to the world," He prayed to the Father, "anymore than I belong to the world. Consecrate them in the truth; your word is truth. As you sent me into the world, I have sent them into the world" (John 17:16-18). Every Christian has been filled with God and then sent into the world to bring that Lord and Savior to it. The Holy Spirit within Christians flows out of those Christians, touching the lives of everyone around them.

Jesus explained what would happen when that Spirit began to live in the soul and the soul began to live in the Spirit. A union with God would result—a union so powerful, so simple, and so sublime that no one could come within its proximity and not be affected by it.

"With me in them and you in me, may they be so completely one that the world will realize that it was you who sent me and that I have loved them as much as you loved me, Father" (John 17:23). The Trinity—three Persons in one God—is a community, a family. God is love, and that love extends Itself in the Christian and in turn, must extend Itself to the world—the Family in the Trinity and the Trinity in the Family.

Jesus gives us the reason for this: "so that the love with which you loved me may be in them and so that I may be in them." It is an awesome reality, a terrible responsibility—the Christian possesses in his soul, through the Holy Spirit, the same kind of love with which the Father loves the Son! Since we are made in His image, possess His Spirit, and are filled with His love, this creates within the soul a family spirit: a concern for others, a desire to diffuse goodness, a capacity to love, a new strength to sacrifice, an ability to bear fruit a hundredfold.

Within the individual soul there is the Family of Persons —a need to share, to give, to radiate, to express concern. There is no longer an isolated individual, seeking self alone, but a togetherness—the soul and the Trinity—one in will, in purpose, in love.

"On that day you will understand," Jesus told the Apostles, "that I am in the Father and you in me and I in you" (John 14:20). This dependence of the soul on God for its life, breath, and joy creates a need to give as one is given. As the soul feels itself being filled, it desires to give itself to others in the same unselfish way it is receiving from God its Father. Family Spirit is born within the soul and that Spirit extends itself to everyone, everywhere, in every facet of everyday life. A constant source of unending love is poured forth from the soul and God together. A spark is kindled within cold hearts, harmony restored where dissension once reigned, faith where cynicism and unbelief were masters.

How true are the words Jesus spoke to us when He said, "Whoever remains in me, with me in him, bears fruit in plenty" (John 15:5). We were created in His Image, and that image is not only in our intellectual faculties, but in the harmony of the life of the Trinity. Sin destroyed that harmony. Man decided to stand alone, outside the influence of the Trinity—the Three in one God.

The more man rebelled, the further away he went from harmony and family spirit. No matter how hard he tried, man and God were on a Creator-creature basis — servant of the Great Yahweh. But the Father sent His Son and when the "Word was made flesh and dwelt among us" — when He died and rose, He bestowed on us the gift of gifts — an opportunity to be part of God's family. Jesus, our brother, God our Father, the Spirit our Indweller.

"I shall not call you servants anymore," Jesus said, "because a servant does not know his master's business; I call you friends, because I have made known to you everything I have learnt from my Father" (John 15:15). "Anyone who does the will of my Father in heaven, he is my brother and sister and mother" (Matt. 12:50). Doing the Father's Will is to be a child of the Father. The Spirit of Jesus in us inspires, leads, and bestows a greater participation in the very Nature of God every time we choose His Will over ours, every time we prefer our Family of Persons (the Trinity) to ourselves. This constant giving and receiving on the part of God and the soul is at the core of the family spirit within us. As we habituate ourselves to this type of family living we spread this spirit to others. As God is the initiator of goodness in our regard, we become the initiators of goodness in the lives of others. As God loves us because He is good, so we love our neighbor out of that infinite source of goodness within us.

We are able then to be self-effacing, prefer the good of others to ourselves, do good to those who persecute us, and forgive seventy times seven. We can truly be compassionate as our Father is compassionate and merciful as He is merciful because our family life with the Trinity has enabled us to love in the same way God loves.

Family living has also suffered on a Parish level. It is a place in which we are baptized, confirmed, taught, cleansed, married, and buried. The Parish can become the family "batter board." Because it represents God, we blame it when things go wrong, criticize it when it does not share our opinions, and condemn it when it falters. The result can be a parish that houses factions, referees dissensions, and spends precious time merely keeping the boat from capsizing. There is no progress forward to give courage, or digression backward to signal danger. Families become statistics, wage earners categorized as givers or nongivers, workers or nonworkers. Shepherd and sheep end up matching wits to survive.

Family living on the national level is shaky and uncertain. Leaders are mistrusted, political office has become synonymous with cheating, bribery, and lies. Sinful enterprises are condoned under the guise of freedom. Abortion and euthanasia are mere debates over heated questions. Political pressure rather than a deep desire for the right to life, ultimately decides the answer, formulates laws, and rationalizes sin. Fear of the decisions of those in office creates a cold war between governments and the citizens of those governments. The integrity, honesty, justice, and wisdom of those in office are held in question, and then it is that both faith and hope in the nation waver. Love grows cold and with it loyalty.

The Religious Family has also suffered in this day of enlightenment. The security of that life is uncertain. Religious no longer feel bound together by the ties of the vows and mutual commitment. There is a new freedom that fills the soul with the cold chill of indifference to each other, to the aged and sick members, to the apostolate and to retirement. Disappointment and heartache dig deep into some hearts while others fear the future of the order they loved so dearly. Confusion over priorities and values causes dissension, and complicated solutions produce burdens too heavy to carry. The constant changing of theological views and opinions shakes whatever semblance of stability remains. Vocations begin to waver. Hard-hearted rebellion against good changes or necessary modifications causes untold harm. The religious family loses togetherness and the sense of belonging.

The Family Spirit in our souls will result in ennobling and building up the family spirit in our life at home, in our community, in our parish and nation. In proportion as we are alienated from the family spirit in our soul, in that degree we are at enmity with our brother. Our relationship with our neighbor will be either close, distant, or indifferent. Only when we live within the warmth of God's unselfish love can we invite others to come in from the cold.

Nations do not fall except when families have ceased to live in a family spirit. It is also true that members of families are not alienated from each other except when each member decides to stand alone outside of God's family. Since he was made in that Image, only by living and growing in that Image can he possibly bear the fruit of harmony and unity.

"I am the vine, you are the branches. Whoever remains in me, with me in him, bears fruit in plenty" (John 15:5).

We see the emergence of this family spirit immediately after Pentecost. Before Pentecost the Apostles and disciples were individuals called together to do a work. When the test came at the Crucifixion, each ran his own way. After the Resurrection and Ascension they stayed together, but more out of fear than love.

When they received the Spirit of Jesus into their very souls, they became family—brothers. There was an invisible bond between them that neither trial, persecution, personality clashes, nor differences of opinions could diminish. Deep in the heart of each one that possessed the Holy Spirit, the goal was the imitation of Jesus. This oneness of heart made them one in mind. They saw God in everything that happened to them, depended upon Him for everything they needed, and prayed to Him for each other. The personality clashes that disturbed and caused dissension before, now became only opportunities to die to self, be understanding, and imitate Jesus. They treated all men as brothers, and that is why St. Peter could say, "For the sake of the Lord, accept the authority of every social institution.... God wants you to be good citizens.... Have respect for everyone and love the community; fear God and honor the emperor" (1 Pet. 2:13, 15, 17). The Family Spirit among the first Christians touched the whole world, and it was that spirit of togetherness, love, and respect that witnessed to the world that Jesus was Lord Messiah.

Prayer

O Holy Trinity, let me live within You that we may share and speak as friend speaks to friend. Let our union of mind and heart, through the power of Your Spirit, enable me to live as one with You. Let the power of that union touch the hearts of everyone around me so all may share in our harmony together in Your Spirit. Let my family, community, parish, and nation live within and grow in this family spirit so the world may know Jesus is Lord and that Your love embraces all mankind. Amen. So be it.

In Praise of Goodness

When historians glance back at this twentieth century, they will primarily see two things: great advances in science and great sin. At no other time has man taken such giant strides forward and backward at the same time. The perplexing aspect of this phenomenon is that it is unobserved by so many. For in our backward swing, we have gone beyond years and reached the animal levels. At the same time we have gone forward with a technology that can press a button and direct a missile thousands of miles away—send voices on laser beams and pictures on satellites.

The impact of such a forward-backward living tears apart the identity of the human nature God has given us. We resemble computers intellectually and animals emotionally. We are like children playing games, with only the fun involved as our goal. When the fun is gone, we either change games or hang our heads in a bored pout as we await the next thrill to come along.

Lethargy is another evil of our day. There are many who are not guilty of doing anything wrong, but very guilty of sins of omission, the things they neglect to do—the good things—the kind, thoughtful words, compassionate thoughts and hopeful attitudes they might have had towards their neighbor. This promotes a lack of zeal for the Church and God's Kingdom. At first sight one might think this is not important, but it is. Without this inner power that makes us care—makes us indefatigable in our efforts to change, strong in our Christian principles, our faith, and our morals—we are open and vulnerable to every kind of worldly temptation, false doctrine, and evil desire. We are like "reeds shaken by the wind" (Matt. 11:7), without purpose, goal, or zeal.

St. Paul draws a graphic picture of what happens when we let ourselves go on in this listless and aimless fashion.

"They knew God and yet refused to honor him as God or to thank him; instead they made nonsense out of logic and their empty minds were darkened. The more they called themselves philosophers, the more stupid they grew" (Rom. 1:21). The consequences of spiritual inertia are tragic and St. Paul saw these results just as we do today. "God left them," he told the Romans, "to their filthy practices ... degrading passions, monstrous behavior ... stupid in all sorts of depravity, greed, envy, malice, men turning from natural intercourse to being consumed with passion for each other, libelers, rebellious to parents and enterprising in sin" (Rom. 1:26-32).

This letter of Paul reads like today's newspaper. Times have not changed, but they should have. Human beings still insist on living on the degrading level of uncontrolled passions and vice, but God desires to do now as He did then, and that is to inspire Christians to go against the trends of the day and be virtuous.

Today's man of the world proclaims that sin, and his enterprising in sin, are a part of modern living, but it is not modern. It goes back to Adam and Eve: to desire and the temptation to know, to experience evil. The problem with this old deception is that the knowledge of evil blots out the desire for good. Evil slowly enwraps the soul with the fine silk threads of self-indulgence. As each thread takes hold, it is only a matter of time before the soul is deaf, dumb, and blind to virtue, goodness, and God. It is then that the rest of Paul's letter becomes a reality, for they are "without brains, honor, love, or pity."

Man can and does rationalize his sins. He finds reasons for all his weakness, invents excuses that first calm and then deaden his conscience. He blames God, society, education, and environment for his wrongdoing. If his conscience manages to survive this barrage of reasoning, he then allows himself the broad excuse of modern living—new concepts of morality and intellectual superiority over those who lived before him. This latter type of excuse deals the final death-blow to his conscience. The acceptance of sin by the majority leads the soul into limitless realms of self-indulgence, for human respect, imperfect motive though it be, is pushed aside by human acceptance. All the weaknesses that were once controlled by prayer and God's grace, plow through the soul like a tornado in an empty field, swirling round and round, rooting up the flowers of virtue, the fruit of hard work and the soil of goodness. The soul becomes a maze of wrecked dreams, twisted goals, and crushed ambitions. It is now that the soul finally becomes enslaved by uncontrolled passions, and the dark silence of despair falls upon it.

"When self-indulgence is at work," Paul wrote to the Galatians, "the results are obvious: fornication, gross indecency and sexual irresponsibility; idolatry and sorcery; feuds and wrangling, jealousy, bad temper and quarrels; disagreements, factions, envy, drunkenness, orgies and similar things" (Gal. 5:19-21). Here we see human nature at its worst, giving in to every inclination for pleasure. We do not often think of disagreements, factions, bad temper, quarrels, and jealousy as a self-indulgent weakness, but when we look more closely we find selfishness as the basis for these sins. We become conceited, self-opinionated, self-willed, domineering. These put emphasis and values on the gratification of our own feelings, reasoning, and will; the three faculties of the soul become completely engrossed within themselves, leaving God and neighbor outside. What is the remedy for such a condition of heart and soul? Is it possible in this world of self-indulgence to take a stand against the general trend? Yes, Jesus came for this very purpose. The Spirit He sent us and the grace He merited for us can give us the courage and strength to withstand the world and all its enticements.

St. Paul, as he spoke to the Colossians about their impurity, greed, and evil desires said, "This is the way in which you used to live when you were surrounded by people doing the same thing, but now, you, of all people, must give up these things: getting angry, being bad tempered, spitefulness, abusive language and dirty talk....You have stripped off your old behavior with your old self, and you have put on a new self which will progress towards knowledge the more it is renewed in the image of its Creator" (Col. 3:7-10).

How great is the mercy of God. He not only hounds us to repent, but gives us a whole new creation within our souls. Such a change does repentance spark, that the soul grows into a clear image of its Creator; from a life of misery, hopelessness, slavery, and guilt, to one of joy, trust, freedom, and self-control. Darkness gives way to light, passion to virtue, sadness to joy.

We are well aware of the effect of evil upon our souls. Perhaps we need to meditate on the necessity of goodness, so we may choose the right course and fulfill the purpose of our creation.

A Clean Memory — Purity of Heart

The faculty of the soul that we call Memory is the one most worked upon by the world, the flesh, and the devil. The Memory is like a computer—it stores everything that passes through the five senses. It takes these impressions and enhances them by the imagination and the results can be tragic if we are not discerning. Jesus told His disciples, "It is from within, from men's hearts, that evil intentions emerge: fornication, theft, murder, adultery, indecency, pride, folly. All these evil things come from within and make a man unclean" (Mark 7:20-23).

We must be very careful about what we allow to enter this computer, for it cannot easily be erased. Today the world has left nothing undone to obtain the mastery of the memory level of every man, woman, and child. Everywhere one goes, there is a barrage of evil seeking to be stored in the memory. Billboards, advertisements, TV, newspapers, radios, and songs are being more and more geared towards "sexual irresponsibility, violence, prejudice, disobedience and rebellion"—all of which are stored in the memory, always ready for the Enemy to bring out, place before us, and tempt us to act more on an animal level than on a reason level. If our Faith in God is weak, our hope wavering, and our love for Him cold, we become easy prey for the attacks of the world, the flesh, and the devil. This is the reason so many men, destined to be sons of God, lower themselves to degrading levels, live for pleasure alone, and seldom do what is reasonable. Jesus describes this plight when He asked us to judge a tree by its fruit. "A man's words flow out of what fills his heart. A good man draws good things from his store of goodness; a bad man draws things from his store of badness" (Matt. 12:34-35).

As children of God it is our happy privilege to radiate the goodness of our Father. This necessitates the obligation of seeing that nothing enters the faculty made to His image that in any way mars or distorts that image.

Our Memory must be compassionate towards those who have hurt us so we harbor no resentments, free of any recollection that makes us lose our self-control. Like an empty jar, it can only feed back what we in turn have fed it. Our Christian principles and the following of Jesus will fill this faculty with good things — forgiving thoughts, compassionate understanding, and purity of heart. Hope will replace despair, and joy, sadness. The fresh air of God's grace will replace the sickening stench of evil as the garbage of bad thoughts disintegrates before the fire of His Love.

A Clean Intellect — Purity of Mind

Whatever we feed our Memory is absorbed by our Intellect. Reason separates, divides, analyzes, forms opinions and makes decisions. It is here we arrive at a set of values and priorities. If we permit ourselves to live on a Memory level only, then our values drop almost to the "instinct" level or we set our goals on values that are passing, unimportant, or imaginary. We see everything on a selfish level, judge everything only by its effect on us, work only for our own good and have little or no regard for our neighbor. Cruelty, disobedience, and rudeness take possession of a faculty that was given to us by God to raise us above every other animal. As a result, man can do things that animals without reason would never do.

Jesus came that we might live on a higher level — the level of Faith. He became man and suffered from the cruelty of other men so we would rise above this world and follow in His footsteps. He wants us to live, not by the things we see, but by the things we do not see. He told us that His Father was our Father; His Spirit lives in our souls. His Love is preparing a place for us in His Father's House.

We need not fear trials, suffering, poverty, or pain, for He had them all and overcame them. He gave us Beatitudes to live by and these principles rise above our human reason. He told us that the "poor in spirit would possess a kingdom," while human reason says they possess nothing. He said the "gentle inherit the earth," but reason says they lose it and only the violent possess the earth. He promised that those who "mourn for their sins would be comforted," but reason says there is no use crying over the past. Those who thirst for holiness would be satisfied, He told the Apostles, but human reason says it is better to seek worldly gain in the here and now.

The "merciful" were promised mercy and the "pure of heart" the sight of God, but human reason says you can carry forgiveness too far and purity is a virtue of the past.

He held "peacemakers" in high regard, called them "sons of God," but human reason calls them "busybodies or fools" who get involved in other people's business.

To the world the most "unreasonable beatitude of all is the one where Jesus expects His followers to "rejoice and be glad when they are persecuted and abused for His sake for their reward would be great in heaven" (Matt 5:1-12). The world cannot accept loss as gain. It is easy to see that if we live by human reason alone we shall be bogged down by a thousand legitimate reasons for living an enslaved miserable life. It is only those glorious Beatitudes that raise us above and beyond our human reason to the freedom of sons of God.

A Clean Soul — Purity of Will

As our Memory presents us with what to choose and our Intellect discerns how and why, it is the Will that accomplishes, performs, and does. This power can say yes or no even to God. It is an awesome power, given by an Awesome God. As the Will goes, the soul goes, and that is why we see Jesus constantly directing us to the accomplishment of the Father's Will over our own. His own life was lived only to do the Father's Will. He called that will His "food." He was anxious to accomplish it and told us over and over that He "only did what He saw the Father do and only said what He heard the Father say" (John 5:19; 8:28).

He promised us that if we did the Father's holy and perfect Will, we would be like a "mother, brother and sister" to Him (Matt. 12:50). He will not force us to give Him this prized possession; He wants it from us freely and out of love. It is only the world, the flesh, and the Enemy that use force to possess our Will. To accomplish this, the world uses enticements, the flesh uses passions, and the Enemy uses deception. All of these allurements are powers that coerce and force the will of man in the direction of evil. The mind is confused and unable to see the right choice clearly. Only God permits man to choose freely, by presenting him with grace, light, and love, all of which produce the clarity of thought and mind so necessary for a wise choice. There is none of the confusion, anxiety, and frustration so present to the soul as when the will is influenced by evil.

The accomplishment of that Holy Will is not always easy; it was not so, even for Jesus. However difficult it is, we may be sure it is far less difficult than the frustration of choosing any other will. The choice of evil over good is always more painful than the momentary pain of self-control.

We were created out of Love, by Love in order to love. We are out of place and misfits when we try to be anything else than what we were created to be — good, loving, joyful, compassionate, kind, understanding, chaste, and holy, "holy as our heavenly Father is holy."

We will grow in Hope as our Memory is filled with mercy, and we will grow in Faith as our Intellect is filled with humility. Then it is that our Will, united to His, will grow in Love, for the "virtuous will shine like the sun in the kingdom of their Father" (Matt. 13:43).

Mother M. Angelica
(1923–2016)

Mother Mary Angelica of the Annunciation was born Rita Antoinette Rizzo on April 20, 1923, in Canton, Ohio. After a difficult childhood, a healing of her recurring stomach ailment led the young Rita on a process of discernment that ended in the Poor Clares of Perpetual Adoration in Cleveland.

Thirteen years later, in 1956, Sister Angelica promised the Lord as she awaited spinal surgery that, if He would permit her to walk again, she would build Him a monastery in the South. In Irondale, Alabama, Mother Angelica's vision took form. Her distinctive approach to teaching the Faith led to parish talks, then pamphlets and books, then radio and television opportunities.

By 1980 the Sisters had converted a garage at the monastery into a rudimentary television studio. EWTN was born. Mother Angelica has been a constant presence on television in the United States and around the world for more than thirty-five years. Innumerable conversions to the Catholic Faith have been attributed to her unique gift for presenting the gospel: joyful but resolute, calming but bracing.

Mother Angelica spent the last years of her life cloistered in the second monastery she founded: Our Lady of the Angels in Hanceville, Alabama, where she and her Nuns dedicated themselves to prayer and adoration of Our Lord in the Most Blessed Sacrament.